ENOUGH

Discovering a God Who Is Enough *When You're Not*

D1602406

TAMYRA HORST

Pacific Press®
Publishing Association

Nampa, Idaho | www.pacificpress.com

Cover design by Gerald Lee Monks
Cover design resources from iStockPhoto.com | recep-bg
Inside design by Aaron Troia

The author assumes full responsibility for the accuracy of all facts and quotations as cited in this book.

Additional copies of this book are available for purchase by calling toll-free 1-800-765-6955 or by visiting adventistbookcenter.com.

Library of Congress Cataloging-in-Publication Data

Names: Horst, Tamyra, 1961- author.
Title: Enough : discovering a God who is enough when you're not Tamyra Horst.
Description: Nampa, Idaho : Pacific Press Publishing Association, 2019. | Summary: "Lessons from Bible characters as well as life experiences that teach us that God is always enough" — Provided by publisher.
Identifiers: LCCN 2019051745 | ISBN 9780816366224 | ISBN 9780816366231 (kindle edition)
Subjects: LCSH: Christian women—Religious life. | God (Christianity)—Biblical teaching. | Self-esteem—Religious aspects—Christianity. | Confidence—Religious aspects—Christianity. | Christian life.
Classification: LCC BV4527 .H665 2019 | DDC 248.8/43—dc23
LC record available at https://lccn.loc.gov/2019051745

January 2020

Dedication

Dedicated to Kaleigh, one of God's beautiful and chosen princesses. I am praying God's love for you and that His intentional plan for your life is the foundation that give you strength and courage for the amazing adventure that He has planned for you. He is enough.

Contents

Introduction 7

Part 1: The Battle

Chapter 1: Once Upon a Time 11
Chapter 2: Not Enough 16
Chapter 3: The Enemy 24
Chapter 4: The Impact on Our Lives 33
Chapter 5: The Impact on Our Relationships 42

Part 2: The Lie, the Truth, and a Big Enough God

Chapter 6: The Lie 55
Chapter 7: The Truth 60
Chapter 8: The God 63
Chapter 9: The Pursuit 70

Part 3: Discovering the Enoughness of God

Chapter 10: The One Thing Needed 81
Chapter 11: The Incredible Gift 92
Chapter 12: Stepping Into God's Big Things 102
Chapter 13: The Story We Tell Ourselves 111
Chapter 14: When We've Blown It 124
Chapter 15: Peace That Passes Understanding 136
Chapter 16: There Will Be Days 145
Chapter 17: One Day Very Soon 154

Invitation 159

Introduction

know firsthand the battle of feeling that you are not enough or are too much—and sometimes both at the same time.

I grew up feeling like I was not enough:

- not good enough
- not pretty enough
- not smart enough
- not talented enough
- not fun enough
- not cool or popular enough
- not thin enough
- not outgoing enough

At the same time, I felt like I was too much:

- too sensitive or emotional
- too fearful
- too quiet
- too talkative sometimes
- too full of ideas
- too animated

These messages came from people I loved, peers, bullies, and mass media. (Even years ago, the mass media bombarded us with images of what we were supposed to look like, be like, or do in order to be—I'm not sure—good enough, perfect, successful, accomplished, and people everyone would want to be friends with.)

My feelings of not being enough caused me to believe that no one would want to be my friend and that no guy would ever be interested in me. They caused me to settle for less, hide out, and avoid trying. The battle followed me into adulthood, where I felt I was not enough as a parent, as a wife, and as a church leader. It made me try harder, work more, and do whatever I could to be enough.

And I'm not alone.

Throughout my thirty-plus years in women's ministries and in my friendships with other women, I know the battle to feel like we are enough, or good enough, is real and constant for many of us. We try hard to be enough—or not too much. Working hard, we constantly watch ourselves to measure how we're doing. Sometimes we give up and hide out and figure we'll never be enough, so why bother trying? We hide in busyness, food, or mass media, or we act like we just don't care, even when we do care.

God and I have journeyed together through this battle. I've learned to turn to Him for the truth about me—the good and the not so great. He's taught me much. I now live with more confidence and peace than I ever have. There are days when the "not enoughness" threatens to take out my heart by discouraging me, causing me to lose hope and give up. But I've learned to turn to Him and remind myself of what He says and who I am in Him. I brush myself off and keep moving forward with the confidence that He has begun a work in me and He will be faithful to complete it (see Philippians 1:6).

For years, I told women that not being enough is a lie of the enemy who wants to destroy us and keep us from being who God created us to be and living the life He created us to live. Then, a couple of years ago, I realized that it is true—we are not enough, never will be, and can't be on our own, no matter how hard we try. (And we try.) I realized the real lie is that we have to be enough—that *we* have to make ourselves enough.

The truth is that God is enough. He longs for us to discover Him in our not enoughness. It's deepened my journey with Him and given me new hope and courage. I've learned a lot through the years and am continuing to learn and grow. I don't believe we ever arrive at the point where we live as though we feel we are enough and are invincible. But I live with confidence more often than defeat. And when I am discouraged or defeated, I don't stay there for as long as I once did.

I'm one of those women who love to share what I'm learning from God, especially the things that inspire and impact me the most. I long to see others experience the joy and peace and hope He brings and begin to believe more and more every day that they are loved, chosen, delighted in, wanted, and accepted and that they have an important role to play in this world. You, my friend, were created for so much! You were made to impact the world around you. So thank you for picking up this book and joining me on this journey. I am praying for you and praying that God uses my story, my words, and the lessons I've learned to help you believe and live enough in Him.

Part 1

The Battle

Finally, my brethren, be strong in the Lord and in the power of His might. Put on the whole armor of God, that you may be able to stand against the wiles of the devil. For we do not wrestle against flesh and blood, but against principalities, against powers, against the rulers of the darkness of this age, against spiritual hosts of wickedness in the heavenly places. Therefore take up the whole armor of God, that you may be able to withstand in the evil day, and having done all, to stand.

Stand therefore, having girded your waist with truth, having put on the breastplate of righteousness, and having shod your feet with the preparation of the gospel of peace; above all, taking the shield of faith with which you will be able to quench all the fiery darts of the wicked one. And take the helmet of salvation, and the sword of the Spirit, which is the word of God; praying always with all prayer and supplication in the Spirit, being watchful to this end with all perseverance and supplication.
—Ephesians 6:10–18

The battle is closer than we realize.

Chapter 1

Once Upon a Time

She burst into the room wearing a princess dress. "Look at me; I'm a princess!" she declared with joy as she twirled and danced.

I don't remember how old my niece Kaleigh was at the time. I wish I had taken pictures. She soon disappeared and then reappeared in a different princess dress but with the same exuberance and joy. The innocent little girl was sure that everyone in the room loved her and would delight in and celebrate her.

"Look at me; I'm a princess!" she sang again as she began twirling. There's just something about twirly skirts for little girls! They just make you want to dance and twirl and enjoy. (Who hasn't twirled in a skirt, even if no one was watching?) The singsong declaration and dancing lasted a minute before Kaleigh was off down the hall to her room to change into another princess dress.

By the third or fourth grand entrance and twirling declaration of her royal status, her dad started to tell her to stop. I interrupted him. "Don't tell her to stop. The world will tell her she's not a princess soon enough. Let her enjoy it and believe it for now."

No longer princesses

As I write this, Kaleigh is thirteen, and her perspective is changing. Instead of twirling, she changes outfits several times because nothing looks right. No longer declaring she's a princess, she's too often focused on what isn't right about herself and her appearance. This breaks my heart. She's a beautiful, creative, and thoughtful girl. She's strong and persistent and caring. She helps me with princess teas and other parts of my ministry whenever she can. She can be shy and introverted; she recently told me that she was tired of interacting with the friendly people at a church where I was speaking and was ready to leave. Like most girls her age, she's a complex mix of emotions and thoughts—sometimes jumping from one to another without any warning for unsuspecting parents.

Last summer I had the incredible honor of baptizing her as she made her commitment to God public. Family and friends gathered on the banks of a lake our families have kayaked together. As the sun set and our friends headed home, she asked me to go out in the kayaks with her. This is a memory I will always treasure. I long for her to always see herself as beautiful inside and out, strong, creative, and caring—the way I see her.

But the transition from little girl to teen is hard. And it impacts girls in so many ways:

- hormonally
- emotionally
- feeling pressured to fit in while also standing out
- taking advanced-placement classes
- taking college-credit courses while still in high school
- participating in sports
- feeling the need to be thin enough, pretty enough, and wear just the right clothes

Social media adds a new level to the pressure—even when you know that many "perfect" pictures have filters on them.

"Then you think you should look that way with filters too," a seventeen-year-old girl recently shared with me as we talked about the battles and pressures that she and her friends face daily. Suddenly, who you are isn't enough. There's pressure to grow up and be perfect, look perfect, and do everything not only well but to excel. It's no wonder that anxiety and depression are at an all-time high and growing, especially among teen girls.

Ypulse, a polling firm that focuses on Generation Z and millennials, surveyed more than thirteen hundred girls, ages eight to eighteen, on the topic of confidence. The results were dramatic.

- There was a 30 percent drop in confidence during puberty.
- The number of girls who said they were not allowed to fail rose from 18 percent to 45 percent from the ages of twelve to thirteen (that's a 27-percent increase in just one year!).
- Girls under twelve shared that they "make friends really easily. [They] . . . can go up to anyone and start a conversation." By the age of fourteen, they reported, "I feel like everybody is so smart and pretty and I'm just this ugly girl without friends."[1]

Many girls do not believe they are good enough. One report states that "7 in 10 girls believe they are not good enough or do not measure up in some way, including their looks, performance in school and relationships with family and friends."[2]

This lack of confidence causes girls to avoid taking risks or trying new things and keeps them from believing that God has a plan for their lives. They do not believe that who they are and what they are good at are acceptable. They often tend to try to please everyone around them (parents, teachers, friends, boys), and they expect perfection from themselves. And no matter how hard those who love them try to encourage them and tell them they're still princesses, these girls no longer believe it.

Feeling like they're not good enough often causes girls to focus on negative feelings and thoughts. Their brains become hardwired to think negatively.

Each thought creates a path in the brain. The more we think that thought, the stronger the path. For instance, you look in the mirror and think, *I'm fat.* A path is created. The next time you look in a mirror, your brain remembers and thinks, *I'm fat.* You accept that thought, and the path deepens. Soon every time you look in the mirror, you see someone who is fat without even thinking about it—no matter what you really look like. (How many of us have looked back at pictures of ourselves when we were younger and thought we were fat only to realize we weren't?) The path becomes a deep rut in your thinking.

It becomes the truth of who we are in our minds: *I'm not good enough.*

It's not just little girls

These deep ruts of negative thinking follow us into our adult lives. They become so ingrained in how we see ourselves that we refuse to believe anything anyone says to the contrary. No matter how many successes, accomplishments, or changes we make, we continue to see ourselves as not good enough.

We grow up into women who no longer twirl around rooms, singing about being princesses. Instead, we look into mirrors and see more things wrong with ourselves than right. We walk into rooms sometimes hoping no one will notice us.

How did we get here?

I'm not sure I remember ever feeling like a princess. I don't remember dancing and twirling in front of people who laughed, celebrated me, and said, "Yes, you are a princess!" I do remember cartwheeling everywhere one summer. I can remember one day when I tried to see how many cartwheels I could do without stopping. (I think I got to more than 100.) I also remember hearing someone say afterward, "That girl can't just walk anywhere. She always has to be cartwheeling."

In my young mind, it sounded like cartwheeling wasn't good, and I internalized the message that I needed to be quieter, calmer, and not quite so animated. I just wasn't quiet enough. It wasn't the first not-enough message and definitely wouldn't be the last. Yet it made my little-girl heart believe I needed to tone down my exuberance for life and be quieter and calmer, to blend in and not stand out.

Children are young and impressionable. They learn about life and who they are from the people around them. They long to be loved and accepted. They don't have the life experience to understand people and why they say and do the things they do. They listen and watch people in their lives, interpreting their words and responses to them as the truth of who they are.

Katie still remembers the day she was singing, and her mom told her, "Stop that awful racket." Her little-girl heart heard, "You can't sing well enough." And for a long time, she didn't sing out loud with people around. "Looking back, I realize that we were in the car. Everyone was making noise. Mom was tired. Maybe she was talking to all of us—not just me singing. But I didn't understand that at the time. I just thought my singing must be pretty bad. So I stopped singing when people were listening."

The messages come from a variety of places. Each of our stories is different. And we all believe that we're not enough (or too much) in different ways or in distinct areas of our lives. Our stories have been impacted by people—parents, teachers, coaches, strangers, relatives, friends, and middle-school bullies. As we grow, the list of people who speak into our lives includes bosses, boyfriends, and husbands, even our children. But it's not just people. How we interpret our failures, not-so-great grades, and mistakes shapes how we see ourselves. The media we take in shapes not only our worldview but also our personal view. Magazine covers with thin, beautiful women (next to the "best chocolate-cake recipe you have to try!") cause us to see ourselves as not thin or pretty enough. Social media has drastically increased the messages we receive as we view others' Instagram-filtered photos and glimpse their fun vacations and outings with friends, which we weren't invited to! All too often our social-media scrolling leaves us feeling discontent, left out, and as though we are not enough.

Many of the messages were never meant to hurt us. Some impacted us because of our interpretation of them. As kids, we tend to make messages about ourselves, even when they have nothing to do with us. Mom and Dad divorce. Dad drinks too much and gets angry. Mom is emotionally distant and doesn't have time to play or listen. An authority figure abuses us. A child may blame himself or herself: "If only I were a better kid, this wouldn't happen."

There are also people in our lives who did speak words to punish us and make us feel bad: bullies, angry parents, and abusive spouses. We took in their angry, mean words and allowed them to define us.

None of us walk through life unscathed by messages that wound our hearts and impact how we see ourselves. Is it possible to ever believe we are princesses again? To dance into a room and assume that everyone will be delighted to see us and love us?

Your story

- Do you remember moments when you felt delighted in? Loved? Maybe like a princess?
- What are the messages that told your heart you weren't enough? Do you remember when they began?
- What do you tell yourself when you look in a mirror? When you make a mistake or fail?

God is enough

God is enough to heal the wounds caused by hurtful messages, and He will bring you confidence and peace with who you are in Him.

Promise

"Long before he laid down earth's foundations, he had us in mind, had settled on us as the focus of his love, to be made *whole and holy* by his love" (Ephesians 1:4, *The Message*; emphasis added).

Prayer

Father God, Ruler of the universe, Creator of the heavens and earth and of us, speak hope and courage into our hearts. Bring healing to those places that were wounded by the messages we've heard about ourselves. Give us a willingness to hear and *believe* what *You* say about us. Remind us that You have called us daughters, and that makes us true princesses. Thank You for loving us with a love that longs to make us whole and holy. In Jesus' name, amen.

---

1. Ypulse and Confidence Code for Girls, "The Confidence Code for Girls: The Confidence Collapse and Why It Matters for the Next Gen," Confidence Code for Girls, April 3, 2018, https://static1.squarespace.com/static/588b93f6bf629a6bec7a3bd2/t/5ac39193562fa73cd8a07a89/1522766258986/The+Confidence+Code+for+Girls+x+Ypulse.pdf.

2. Dove Self-Esteem Fund, *Real Girls, Real Pressure: A National Report on the State of Self-Esteem* (Englewood Cliffs, NJ: Dove Self-Esteem Fund, 2008), quoted in "Statistics on Girls & Women's Self Esteem, Pressures & Leadership," Heart of Leadership, January 10, 2014, https://heartofleadership.org/statistics/.

Chapter 2

Not Enough

When I went to kindergarten, my uncle promised to frame my first painting. After I finished, he designed the wooden frame and stained it. He even matted the painting as if it were a fine piece of art. I still have it all of these years later. It is a piece of art, I suppose—abstract art. It is not a scene or object that you can identify.

I've shown the painting to people and asked, "What is this a painting of?" It usually takes a couple of minutes before they even attempt to respond. (Remember, it was painted by a five-year-old who had never painted before, and it looks like I used only one fat brush for all the different colors. And I've always loved color.) No two people have ever guessed the same thing or come close to what I point out in the painting. Even after I share my ideas of what is in the picture, it takes a bit of imagination, or maybe even a lot of imagination, to see it.

So if everyone has a different answer, who is right about what the painting depicts?

Who defines *enough*?

We'll get back to the painting and decide who is right later. But let's ask a more important question. As we struggle to feel good enough (or whatever word you use in place of *good*—*smart, pretty*, etc.), how do we know what *enough* looks like? How will we know when we are finally enough? Who defines what *enough* is? If we're trying so hard to be good enough, shouldn't we know what it looks like so that we'll know we've arrived?

Dictionary.com defines *enough* as "adequate for the want or need; sufficient for the purpose or to satisfy desire"; "in a quantity or degree that answers a purpose or satisfies a need or desire."[1] So being enough is being adequate for the want or need, being sufficient for the purpose for which we were created.

Who gets to define our purpose and decide whether we are sufficient?

Social media? The number of likes on our posts, or the number of followers on our profiles? Strangers who don't know or care about us? Peers at school or work who are not actually our friends but who are the popular people everyone wants to know and hang out with? The scale or the tags in the back of our dresses? Test scores? Our titles or jobs? Our bosses? Pastors? Coworkers? Family and friends? Ourselves?

Reading that list after typing it, I think to myself, *No, social media, strangers, and people who don't know and love me do not get to decide whether I'm enough or not. They don't know me and, honestly, don't care about me. They probably don't even think about me. The scale or size of my clothes doesn't measure my value. My job is what I do, not who I am. It's crazy to let all of those things or people impact how I think about myself.*

But too often, aren't these the places we look to and see that we're not enough?

Do I even trust *myself* to do a good job of deciding whether I'm enough or not? I tend to be overly critical of myself, judging myself much harder than anyone else. My expectations of myself are pretty tough to meet. If I'm honest, I too often expect perfection and have joked that I wish God would just zap me and make me perfect. (It may not really be a joke.) It's too easy for me to dismiss compliments and affirmations from others but hard to forget critical words spoken about me or the things I've done.

Maybe we'll be enough if . . .

When we believe that we're not enough, we are telling ourselves that we don't measure up. We need to be

- smarter
- stronger
- thinner
- friendlier

Or we need to do more:

- accomplish more
- be more successful
- earn more money
- have a better house
- be more involved at church or our kids' school
- work more or work less
- find the perfect balance between work and home and friends

We think, *If only I can do this, then I'll be enough.*

Do you have a list of "if onlys"?

- If only I weighed (insert number) or wore this size.
- If only I were taller (or shorter).
- If only I got this promotion or that job.
- If only I had a boyfriend.
- If only I were married.
- If only I were single.

- If only I lived in that neighborhood.
- If only . . . You get the idea.

A few years ago I was working with a group of middle-school girls. There'd been some challenges with relationships among them, and the tension was beginning to impact the entire school. (It was a small Christian school where everybody knew everyone, and problems in one classroom easily spilled out into the whole building.) The principal knew I had written seminars for teens and asked me to come and talk to the girls in the hope that I could help their relationships and also ease the tension at the school. I began meeting with them monthly for the next two years. In one of our times together, I had them write their "if onlys" on cards. Then they passed the cards to me. Once I had the stack in front of me, I began reading them. (While they were anonymous, it was easy to figure out who had written what.)

- The girl with straight hair wrote, "If only I had curly hair."
- The girl with curly hair wrote, "If only my hair were straight."
- The petite girl wrote, "If only I were taller."
- The tall girl wrote, "If only I were shorter."

I'm not kidding; that's how it went. Each was thinking that what another person had would make them happy and content, while that person saw it as not enough. We laughed a little over the craziness of it and had a good discussion, realizing that if our "if onlys" happened, they might not actually make us feel good enough because they weren't working for other people.

And yet we still long and strive to be enough, even after realizing that the things we think would make us feel like we are enough are the very things that make others feel they are not enough.

So we try harder

We have to do something, right? So we diet. We exercise. We put in more hours at work. We skip vacation to get a project done or take a vacation and stay connected to the office and our to-do list. We read self-help books. We listen to TED Talks. We hire life coaches. Most of these are good things to do, but when seen as a way to become enough, they can actually grow our belief that we're not. Instead, we create new areas where we need to improve and do better.

Our pursuit of being enough is good for the economy.

- "According to the latest IHRSA [International Health, Racquet & Sports-club Association] report, total fitness industry revenue was an estimated $94bn [billion] in 2018, up from $87.2bn in 2017." "In revenue terms, the fitness industry growth rate is 8.7% globally."[2]
- "The beauty industry is valued at $532 billion and is on a rapid upward

trajectory, according to a new report from retail analytics firm Edited."[3]

- "Up to 50 percent of women are on a diet at any given time, according to Judy Mahle Lutter in her book 'The Bodywise Woman.' Up to 90 percent of teenagers diet regularly, and up to 50 percent of younger kids have tried a diet at some point."[4]
- "American workers accumulated 705 million unused days in 2017, up from 662 million days the year before. 52 percent of employees reported having unused vacation days at the end of 2017. . . . In 2017, Americans forfeited 212 million days, which is equivalent to $62.2 billion in lost benefits."[5]

While the pursuit of being enough is big business, it's not good for our hearts. When we feel we are not enough for too long and let it define us, it changes more than just how we see ourselves in the mirror.

It's about more than just being enough

I've realized that the real battle isn't over being enough. It's much deeper and harder than not being good enough at something or wishing you were thinner—and even more than wishing you were a better mom. The real battle is the shame we feel about ourselves as a result.

Just yesterday I was telling a friend what I felt when I looked in the mirror the other day: *disgust*. As soon as I said the word, I knew it was true. I was disgusted that I lacked the discipline and focus to be more mindful about what I ate and disgusted that I had allowed myself to gain weight and not stay toned. I felt shame at who I was when I looked in the mirror.

That's what shame does. It causes us to let our failures and shortcomings define us. We fail, and shame says we are failures. We disappoint someone, and shame says we are disappointments. Shame changes our focus from *doing* something wrong to the feeling that we *are* something wrong. It turns not being good *at* something into not *being* good enough.

Shame causes us to dislike ourselves, beat ourselves up, and even hate ourselves sometimes. We try to do more and be more to quiet the shame we feel. We try dressing trendily to cover up how we feel about our reflection in the mirror. We work harder and put in more hours at work to cover up the fear that our boss or coworkers will discover that we don't really have what it takes. Our internal dialogue reminds us often, even constantly, of our failures and shortcomings.

God doesn't want us to hate ourselves or beat ourselves up: "The Lord is disappointed when His people place a low estimate upon themselves. He desires His chosen heritage to value themselves according to the price He has placed upon them. God wanted them, else He would not have sent His Son on such an expensive errand to redeem them. He has a use for them, and He is well pleased when they make the very highest demands upon Him, that they may glorify His name. They may expect large things if they have faith in His promises."[6]

God loves us, created us, planned for us, and died for us. He longs for us to see ourselves through His eyes.

I remember clearly standing on a stage before two hundred women, sharing the story of the woman with the issue of blood. It's the powerful story of a woman who for twelve years would have heard over and over that she wasn't enough. In her day, a woman was considered unclean when she had her period. And anything she touched was considered unclean. Once her cycle ended, she could offer a sacrifice and be clean again. Only this woman's bleeding never stopped. Days turned into weeks, weeks into months, and months became years. The Bible tells us that she spent all she had in an attempt to get better "and was no better, but rather grew worse" (Mark 5:26).

Imagine her life. She was considered unclean. No one would touch her. No hugs. No one to hold her when she cried. Friends might have been sympathetic in the beginning, but as the problem persisted, people would have distanced themselves. It was common to believe that when something like this happened, God was punishing you for being a sinful person. People ignored her—or worse, accused her and called her names—in their fear that her disease would rub off on them if they got too close. Friends and people who once loved her avoided her and no longer made eye contact. She spent all she had, so it's possible she no longer had a home or anything to call her own. Physically, her body grew weaker and more depleted while she also struggled emotionally, mentally, and spiritually. Had God really abandoned her? Given up on her?

Then she heard about Jesus. He healed people, raised people from the dead, and loved even the unclean. And she told herself, "If only I can get to Jesus and touch His clothes, I shall be made well." So she pushed through a crowd she shouldn't have been in (she was unclean, and anyone who bumped into her became unclean). Mark tells us that the crowd was so great that it "thronged" Jesus (verse 24). She pushed through, and the crowd pushed her. But somehow, she managed to touch Him. And instantly, she was healed. I imagine her stopping, standing still, and looking down at her healed body in amazement.

Suddenly, the crowd stopped too. Jesus stopped and asked, "Who touched Me?"

Luke writes that everyone denied touching Jesus (Luke 8:45). I picture people abruptly stepping away from Jesus and creating space around Him. Maybe as she stands there in awe of her healing, she is now on the edge of the crowd.

Peter asks, "What are You asking? Everyone is touching You!"

But Jesus knew this touch was different. She didn't just bump into Him. She grabbed onto Him with faith, believing that He could make her well. Jesus "looked around to see her who had done this thing" (Mark 5:32). Maybe at that point, their eyes met. He saw her! No one had seen her in a dozen years. No one had looked at her or made eye contact. No one saw past the disease and unclean state to the person. She fell before Him and told her story. "And He said to her, 'Daughter, be of good cheer; your faith has made you well. Go in peace' " (Luke 8:48).

As I shared the story with the gathered women, I suggested that maybe Jesus said "daughter" twice. Looking into her face, He said it once to her, making sure she knew that He claimed her as His daughter and all that word means when you are well loved, accepted, delighted in, and in the place where you belong. And then, He said it a second time, fiercely to the crowd who may have wanted to accuse, hurt, or criticize her for what she had done and how she had made them unclean. "This is My daughter, and don't you mess with her."

As I told the story, I suddenly sensed God speaking to me. *"Tami, who is the person that is the hardest on you?"*

I knew the answer. "Me."

"Don't you mess with My daughter!"

God calls you His daughter. Your earthly father may or may not have done a good job of defining the words *daughter* and *father*, but our Abba in heaven has. Your biological dad may or may not have wanted you or planned for you. But God did. Before you were born, He thought about you and who He wanted you to be. He knit you together—created you specifically—and wrote the story of your life (Psalm 139). He wants you to define yourself by His love.

God's definition of *enough*

Back to the story of my painting and the question of who is right about what the painting depicts. Who is right about what it is a picture of?

Me, of course. I'm the one who painted it. And even if I can't remember what my five-year-old brain was thinking all of those years ago, I am the creator, so I get to define the painting. No one else knows what I was thinking or wanting or attempting to create.

When we apply this idea to ourselves and who gets to define whether or not we are enough, doesn't it seem logical that the One who created us knows our purpose and what He thought when He created us? Isn't God the One who decides whether we're good enough?

What does God think of you?

One of my favorite Bible verses declares, "Long before he laid down earth's foundations, he had us in mind, had settled on us as the focus of his love, to be made whole and holy by his love. Long, long ago he decided to adopt us into his family through Jesus Christ. (What pleasure he took in planning this!) He wanted us to enter into the celebration of his lavish gift-giving by the hand of his beloved Son" (Ephesians 1:4–6, *The Message*).

God began thinking about you before He began creating. He decided then and there that not only would He love you—but you also would be the focus of His love. He would send Jesus to die for you so that He could adopt you and call you daughter for eternity.

He loves you. He thought about you, planned you, and created you.

Do we fail and fall short of His plan?

Yes, but He already knew that (Romans 3:23; 5:8). So He sent His Son to die for us. Now when God looks at us, He sees us through Christ's sacrifice. He doesn't see our sin or failures or the ways we just don't measure up. "Through the righteousness of Christ we shall stand before God pardoned, and as though we had never sinned."[7] Amazing, isn't it? His love is so big that it can be hard to wrap our minds around completely. But if we keep reminding ourselves of this every day, if we allow Him and His love to define us, our perspective will slowly change.

He longs for you and me to believe that we are enough because of Him.

Your story

- Who or what are you allowing to define you and whether you're enough?
- Is it possible that when we feel like we're not enough, we're trying to be people we weren't created to be?
- What are your "if onlys"? Take time to think through what would actually change in your life if they came true. How would they impact the way you saw yourself? Would they really change things as much as you think they might?
- What are the ways you've tried to measure up and be enough? How has that worked out?
- What role has shame played in your journey?
- Take time to think of ways you've beaten yourself up and things you've said to yourself. Confess them to God and ask Him to forgive you for the way you've treated His daughter.

God is enough

God is enough to define and create you. The price He paid for you is enough to define you as valuable and loved.

Promise

For this reason I bow my knees to the Father of our Lord Jesus Christ, from whom the whole family in heaven and earth is named, that He would grant you, according to the riches of His glory, to be strengthened with might through His Spirit in the inner man, that Christ may dwell in your hearts through faith; that you, being rooted and grounded in love, may be able to comprehend with all the saints what is the width and length and depth and height—to know the love of Christ which passes knowledge; that you may be filled with all the fullness of God.

Now to Him who is able to do exceedingly abundantly above all that we ask or think, according to the power that works in us, to Him be glory in the church by Christ Jesus to all generations, forever and ever. Amen (Ephesians 3:14–21).

Prayer

Father God, Abba, the One who sees us, long before we took our first breaths, You thought about us and decided who we would be and how we would impact the world. You carefully chose talents and gifts and passions for us. You decided then and there that You would love us and relentlessly pursue us. Forgive us for allowing other things and people to define us. Forgive us for beating ourselves up and diminishing the beauty You chose for us. God, please heal us of the shame that clouds our perspective. Help us to see and believe Your love a little more each day. Give us the courage to look to You alone to define who we are. In Jesus' name, amen.

1. Dictionary.com, s.v. "enough," accessed November 5, 2019, https://www.dictionary.com /browse/enough.

2. "Fitness Industry Statistics [Growth, Trends & Research Stats, 2019]," Wellness Creative Co., September 2, 2019, https://www.wellnesscreatives.com/fitness-industry-statistics-growth/.

3. Bethany Biron, "Beauty Has Blown Up to Be a $532 Billion Industry—and Analysts Say That These 4 Trends Will Make It Even Bigger," *Business Insider*, July 9, 2019, https://www.business insider.com/beauty-multibillion-industry-trends-future-2019-7.

4. Tammy Dray, "Facts & Statistics About Dieting," LiveStrong, February 25, 2011, https:// www.livestrong.com/article/390541-facts-statistics-about-dieting/.

5. "State of American Vacation, 2018," U.S. Travel Association, May 8, 2018, https://www .ustravel.org/research/state-american-vacation-2018.

6. Ellen G. White, *The Desire of Ages* (Mountain View, CA: Pacific Press®, 1940), 668.

7. Ellen G. White, *Our High Calling* (Washington, DC: Review and Herald®, 1961), 48.

Chapter 3

The Enemy

I love stories: stories of people who have overcome great odds to do amazing things and stories of struggling relationships and of love courageous enough to persevere and not give up. I love stories that end with some degree of happily ever after. And yes, I admit, I am one of those people who reads the end of the book before finishing it; I just need to make sure it's going to end well. I don't want to take the time to read a story that ends badly. And knowing that it all works out helps me to get through the middle part of the story when everything is a mess.

Most great stories have common elements: a hero, an enemy, and a battle to fight.

You and I live in a great story. There's a Hero (hint: it's not us!), an enemy, and a battle to fight.

Ours is a love story. We have a God who loves us and created heaven and earth for us. Stop and think about that for a moment. Picture God—the Father, Son, and Holy Spirit—creating. They spoke, and it was. But imagine the conversations as They spoke flowers into existence—all the different sizes, shapes, colors, and types of flowers. Why so many? Couldn't just a handful be enough? Imagine the conversation as They spoke animals into being. There had to be some crazy discussions; think about giraffes and platypuses. Think about all the different personalities of animals. And why? Because God loves us. He created a world that would reveal Him and His love and His plan. He wanted us to know the peace of sitting on a beach with waves pounding down, calming our hearts and bringing joy. He wanted us to laugh with delight over the antics of an otter or a puppy excited to see us when we come home. He wanted to take our breath away at the beauty and magnitude of mountains. He hid beauty for us to discover and enjoy on mountaintops, in ocean depths, and in the middle of jungles.

No one has ever loved you like He does and has done more for you than He has. I've told my sons often throughout their lives that I love them, but God loves them more. I frequently say that it feels impossible to me that anyone could love them more than I do, but He does. And He wants more for them than I can even imagine. (And now they both have women in their lives who love them more too.)

We have an enemy

But like any good story, we have an enemy. The Bible is very clear. Our enemy has come "to steal and kill and destroy" (John 10:10, NIV). We are warned that he roams around "like a roaring lion, seeking whom he may devour" (1 Peter 5:8).

Steal. Kill. Destroy. Devour.

Why don't we live like it?

How many of us got up this morning thinking, *Today I will have an enemy relentlessly pursuing me to take out my heart and steal my joy and peace. And he will do anything to destroy how I see myself and how I see God?*

I talk about the enemy and the battle often, but too many mornings or days I forget. I don't recognize his attacks. I hear his lies and believe they are the truth about myself, about life, and about people. I forget that I have an enemy seeking to devour me. This enemy wants to destroy my relationships, especially my relationship with God. I have the book *The Great Controversy* on my shelf. It's a book about the battle for our world between God and the enemy down through history. But the great controversy is more than a book or the history of God's people. It's the life we live every day. We just fail to live like it or recognize it.

The enemy likes that we don't think about him or that we make him smaller than he really is. He probably enjoys the cartoon caricature of a devil with horns and a pointy tail. He doesn't want us to think of him as a real threat, and he doesn't want us to look for him and his subtle ways of destroying us.

Often, we think the enemy just wants to tempt us to sin. And he does tempt us to sin. He enjoys getting us to do or think things that we shouldn't. He likes trapping us in addictions and habits that hurt our relationships, influence how we see ourselves, and create barriers between God and us.

But the battle is bigger than that. His desire isn't just to get us to sin but also to take out our hearts—steal, kill, destroy, and devour. I believe he has two goals:

- Keep us from believing we are who God says we are, and keep us from living the life God created us to live.
- Keep us from believing God is who He says He is and that God loves the way He says He loves and will do what He says He will do.

Isn't that what the enemy has been doing from the very beginning? Convincing Adam and Eve that they needed to eat the fruit to really live and be enough? Convincing them that God was holding out on them? And he's been lying to us ever since about who we are and who God is.

Believing the lies

The enemy begins his attack from the moment we're born. He is watching, waiting, and learning about us. Remember, the Bible says he's "like a roaring lion, seeking whom he may devour" (1 Peter 5:8). Think about that imagery. A lion watches, stalks, waits until the moment is right, and then leaps for the kill. Once the enemy finds a weak spot, he relentlessly attacks that area of our hearts over and over.

Have you ever noticed that the messages about not being enough are often in the same areas of your life? In my own life, I've observed that the devil attacks my relationships—or my potential relationships. I love people. I enjoy friendships and getting to know people. These days it's not unusual for me to strike up conversations with strangers when I'm out and about. Just the other day, I asked an older woman whose name tag read "George" whether her name was really George. It turns out it was, and she had been arrested for evading the draft when she was young. The authorities assumed she was a man because of her name.

I love people sharing their stories with me. I've learned most people enjoy talking with me when I ask questions and show interest, so I often look for opportunities to engage people in conversations. It doesn't matter their age. I love chatting with kids as much as, if not more than, adults. I believe everyone has a story to tell and that they want someone to be interested and listen.

But this hasn't always been my story. For too many years, I didn't believe people would want to be my friend and thought no one would be interested in getting to know me or talk with me. Over and over, the enemy had spoken this into my life in a variety of ways, beginning when I was a little girl. I was the shy kid who was never chosen for the kickball team, swinging alone on the swing set or climbing the monkey bars. I was the only girl in a family with four boys who paired off to play together. During high school, a "friend" borrowed my records for a party but didn't invite me; instead, she told me I wouldn't fit in with her friends. The messages I kept hearing over and over as I grew up told me that while I needed to help and take care of everyone, there was no one who was interested in me and no one who wanted to hang out with me and be my friend.

The enemy knew my heart for people and intentionally worked to take out my heart—to tempt me to believe that no one would like me or want to be my friend. I accepted his lies and believed them. I kept busy in the background at events and social gatherings, doing and helping, so I could avoid the loneliness I was sure I'd experience if I attempted to engage.

Often it feels like the truth

The more I accepted the enemy's lies and believed them, the more they seemed to be the truth. Every time I agreed with the temptation to think, *This proves no one wants to be my friend*—instead of looking at the situation or person from a different perspective and asking God to show me what was true—the more I believed that it *was* the truth. No one was interested in me. No one would want to be my friend.

We get to the point that when the enemy lies to us about who we are, we don't recognize it as a lie. It just feels like the truth. We don't question it. We don't take it to God to see what He says. We don't guard our hearts or battle back. We think,

This is just who I am and the way things are.

"No one wants to be my friend."

"I'm fat and ugly."

"I'll never learn. I'm just not smart."

"I can't make a difference."

We allow the enemy to move us slowly from believing a lie in the moment to believing it at the core of who we are. And rarely do we see it coming or recognize that it's the enemy.

Think about how often the negative thoughts come. You drop something and think, *What a klutz!* Next time you drop something or trip or slip, you think, *I am such a klutz!* And slowly, you begin to believe that you are a klutzy person, always dropping things, losing things, or tripping over stuff. It becomes part of how you see yourself—as an ungraceful person. But that is not how God sees you or would talk to you.

The enemy's attacks are often subtle. Think about how many messages you hear about yourself in a day. You get up in the morning and look in the mirror. You have bed head and sleep wrinkles on your face. Forgetting that few people wake up and instantly look beautiful, you look in the mirror and think how unattractive you are. You open the closet to find something to wear to work and instantly think, *I have nothing to wear. Nothing looks good on me.* Just another reminder that you are not beautiful. At work, you pass a colleague who looks great, has cute shoes and a pretty blouse, and you think, *She always looks great. I just look so frumpy.* But you never consider what her inner dialogue is saying to her! She sees you and wishes she could be as efficient and organized as you are; she thinks she'll never be organized enough. You work hard on a project and turn it in to your boss, who doesn't even acknowledge you. The enemy is on a roll as he tempts you to believe the following: *The boss isn't going to like my project. He doesn't think I am up for the task. He probably doesn't even like me and wishes I would quit.* You accept the thought, just as you have all the others throughout the day, and feel discouraged. You think you'll never be enough. You've not considered that the boss is focused on meeting a deadline and is battling his own thoughts of inadequacy. Stopping at the store for a few groceries on your way home, you see the photos of thin, beautiful women on magazine covers while standing at the checkout. Without even thinking about it, you feel even more discouraged as you compare yourself with the Photoshopped images in front of you. By the time you get home and get dinner on the table, you're beating yourself up for not being enough as a mom and feeding your kids a quick meal instead of a home-cooked, healthy meal. Your husband settles in front of the TV, remote in hand, and you wonder whether he's just not that into you anymore. You beat yourself up for not staying in better shape and for putting on a little weight. (All while he's numbing his own discouraging thoughts from work and his role as a dad.) As you fall into bed that night, you realize that you never took the time to hang out with God, and you beat yourself up again. Your last thoughts before you fall asleep are of all the ways you're failing and not measuring up, wondering how long your husband, boss, and God will put up with your inadequacies.

The enemy is celebrating his victories in taking out your heart, and you don't even realize that he was behind it all. In your mind, it was just another day of you being you.

The slippery slide down to shame

Why does the enemy bother with all of these tiny little discouragements? Why doesn't he tempt us to do something big and horrible and take us out that way?

If the enemy could, he would. But most of us would recognize the attack if he were to tempt us to rob a bank or hurt someone. But if he can slowly and daily win these little battles in our thinking, he can move us away from believing we are loved and beautiful, and we were created with a purpose to impact our world. He can cause us to believe that God isn't happy with us and make us doubt His love and His plan.

The enemy will tell us one lie after another as long as we keep accepting them and believing what he says is the truth until we spiral down into shame or despair.

I caught him in the act this summer. I was responsible for a huge event, which had tons of details and moving pieces. It consumed my focus for several weeks, even after months of preparing for it. Things went well—until someone asked me about a video I had completely forgotten. And the person asked me about it on the day it was supposed to be shown. It was too late to film, edit, and produce it. Immediately, I felt like a failure. And the enemy began with his lies: *How could I forget this? It's important for raising the needed funds! I blew it.*

As I accepted the negative, critical thoughts, the enemy moved in for the kill: *I always blow it. I don't have what it takes. I'm just not good at my job.*

That's when I started paying attention to my thoughts and where they were going. The enemy was leading me to shame. I realized that I had just pulled off a more than weeklong event with so many different pieces, including seminars, concerts, and worships. I had planned the details for one of those weeklong worship series, aimed at getting families to worship together, plus oversaw an entire day of family-fun activities. I had organized all the assignments for our team and handled a myriad of small problems that popped up during the week. And I was feeling like a complete failure because I had forgotten one video? A video that others had forgotten too?

"Not today, Satan!" I stopped listening to the lies and stopped believing them. I started looking for the truth. I *had* forgotten that video, but so had the others involved with it, including those it benefited. A mistake for sure, but not the end of the world. And I had stayed on top of so many other things. I wasn't a failure just because of this one mistake.

That's where the enemy wants to take us. One mistake, one failure, or one bad-hair day, and he wants to lead us into shame—lead us into believing we are a mistake, a failure, and have no beauty. The truth is we will all make mistakes, fail, and have bad-hair days. But they do not define us. God defines us. We are who He says we are. We are not our mistakes, our failures, or our bad-hair days.

God will convict us of sin. His convictions lead us to repentance and freedom. They restore us to joy, hope, and courage. The enemy will attempt to cover us in shame, guilt, and discouragement. We cannot let him win. We must remember this is a battle. We must fight. We must guard our hearts.

The Bible promises, "Resist the devil and he will flee from you" (James 4:7). When we start really listening to our thoughts and recognizing where they are coming from—God, ourselves, or the enemy—we can guard our hearts and minds by resisting the enemy. We can say, No, I'm not going to beat myself up like that. I may fail, but I am not a failure. I may disappoint, but I am not a disappointment. I am a much-loved daughter of God, who has forgiven and redeemed my life and created me for a purpose. He has redeemed me, and He sees the beauty in me.

The enemy is afraid of you

Why is the enemy seeking to steal, kill, destroy, and devour you? If you're like me, you don't see yourself as much of a threat to him. I'm just an ordinary woman, attempting to know God, love others, and make a difference in some way in the world—without messing up too much. Why this much hatred and energy? Why try so hard to take out your heart?

Because he is afraid of you.

He knows God created you and loves you. He knows God has given you gifts, talents, and passions. God has a plan for your life and a purpose that will influence the lives of others, causing them to know and believe God's love and redemption in new ways.

He fears what you will do if you live believing you are who God says you are and that God is who He says He is. He knows you would be unstoppable, and others would come to know God in real and undeniable ways.

Yes, you. (Some of you read that last line and thought, *Not me; I'll never make a big difference.*)

The Bible says it's true. We've covered some of this already, but I always appreciate the reminder:

- God decided from the very beginning that we would be the focus of His love, and His goal would be to make us whole and holy (Ephesians 1:4).
- He knew we would sin and fail to measure up, and He made a plan to take care of that (Romans 5:8).
- He designed each of us intentionally, planning our stories (Psalm 139).
- He gave each of us gifts and talents specifically for sharing Him with others (1 Corinthians 12:7).
- He will accomplish His plan in our lives (Philippians 1:6).

Girlfriend, the enemy doesn't want us to live like any of this is true. He knows the difference it would make in us—the peace, the joy, the hope, the courage, and the confidence. He knows the difference it would make in the lives of others: our kids, our husbands, our churches, and our neighborhoods. As women, we impact. We care for others. We nurture and encourage. We are a force when we want to be.

He's afraid, so he is determined to take you out and keep you from all God intended.

Don't let him win. Resist, and he will flee.

Why those messages?

Remember, as we started this conversation about the enemy, I asked you, "Have you ever noticed that the messages about not being enough are often in the same areas of your life?"

Why these areas of your life? Why pound the same message over and over?

I believe it's possible that these are the areas God will use in us to make the most difference in the world. Thus, the focus to take them out.

I also shared the message about not believing anyone would want to be my friend. I heard it in so many ways through the years. It was persistent in my thinking. I'm still often tempted to believe it. Why push so hard to get me to believe that no one would want to be my friend?

Because I care about people. I can be a good friend. I long to encourage others. And not just encourage them when they're struggling, I want to be a woman who believes God has a plan and a dream for other people and do anything I can to help them pursue God's dream. I want to help others believe that God loves them, not just in a head-knowledge way but truly experience it in their everyday lives. My personal mission statement, written in my early thirties and still true today, says, "Encouraging, equipping, and challenging people to love deeply and serve uniquely."

So the enemy attempts to keep me from believing anyone would want to hang with me, talk with me, or listen to me. He wants this belief to cause me to retreat from people, avoid pursuing friendships, and not tell others that God loves them and has an incredible plan for their lives. He doesn't want me to do what God created me to do.

I no longer believe the devil's lies in this area. I know people want someone to believe in them. They need encouragement, and all it takes is listening and treating them with respect, asking questions—no matter how old or young they are. Believing this has opened up opportunities. Just in the last month, I've had two young-adult women ask to hang out with me and talk. Me? I'm old enough to be their mom! I met with one over a cup of tea, talking long after our cups were empty, and another over lunch that lasted all afternoon. One of the personal highlights of the month was when a new coworker showed me her nine-year-old daughter's worksheet from school. They moved here earlier this summer and didn't know people in the area. The coworker's daughters didn't have friends their own age in their new neighborhood. When they visited the office, I made sure to talk to them, ask questions, dig into my supply of crafts from princess teas to give them projects to work on, and showed the nine-year-old the stash of kids' books on my shelves. She began coming to work once a week with her dad and spending the day helping him with small tasks but also hanging out in my office, talking, doing crafts, and reading. When I visited her soon-to-be school and filmed a video, I sent her a photo of her desk with her name on it, ready and waiting, via her dad, and I told her about the bookcase filled with books by the door. One of the first worksheets her teacher had her do was a get-to-know-you type of assignment. Her mom showed me a picture on her phone. The first line read, "My best friend is _____," and she had written, "Tamyra Horst." This brought tears to my eyes! My heart was so touched. A nine-year-old declared me as her best friend. I was humbled and surprised. Her mom encouraged me to keep reading because I was on the sheet in another place. Sure enough, near the bottom, she had filled in another blank: "My favorite place to visit is Tamyra's office."

Way cool! I joked with her dad that he'd thought she was coming to hang with him, but really it was to see me.

If I still believed the enemy's lies, I probably wouldn't have reached out. I may not have accepted the invitations to lunch or tea. I wouldn't talk to strangers and invite them to tell me their stories. I might not travel and speak and meet incredible women who share their stories with me between sessions.

God has created you, my friend, with passions and interests and talents that the enemy will attempt to destroy because he fears what will happen when you live your life believing God instead of him. It's time to take notice of whose voice you're listening to in your head. It's time to resist the enemy and believe God. And it's time to say, "Not today, Satan!" and believe in the beauty God created in you.

Your story

- How aware have you been of the enemy and his attacks on you?
- What are the specific areas in your life where he has attacked over and over?
- What core lies have you believed about yourself and about God?
- How can you pay attention to whose voice you are listening to and resist the enemy's lies? (We'll go over some practical ideas as we journey on through the book.)

God is enough

God is enough to win the battle over the enemy and speak courage and truth into our hearts.

Promise

What, then, shall we say in response to these things? If God is for us, who can be against us? He who did not spare his own Son, but gave him up for us all—how will he not also, along with him, graciously give us all things? Who will bring any charge against those whom God has chosen? It is God who justifies. Who then is the one who condemns? No one. Christ Jesus who died—more than that, who was raised to life—is at the right hand of God and is also interceding for us. Who shall separate us from the love of Christ? Shall trouble or hardship or persecution or famine or nakedness or danger or sword? As it is written:

> "For your sake we face death all day long;
>   we are considered as sheep to be slaughtered."

No, in all these things we are more than conquerors through him who loved us. For I am convinced that neither death nor life, neither angels nor demons, neither the present nor the future, nor any powers, neither height nor depth, nor anything else in all creation, will be able to separate us from the love of God that is in Christ Jesus our Lord (Romans 8:31–39, NIV).

Prayer

Father God, You promise that we are more than conquerors. Yet sometimes we aren't even aware that we're living in a battle or recognize the enemy as real. Open our eyes and ears. Help us to pay attention to our inner dialogues and realize whose voice we are listening to. Give us the strength and courage to resist the enemy and stop believing the lies. Forgive us for not always believing what You say about us. Help us to memorize Your words about who we are and Your plan for us. Give us hope to believe in the dreams You have for us. Father, help us to fight the battle for our hearts—to guard our hearts and minds and allow You to do in and through us more than we can imagine. Heal these wounded places. Break the strongholds we've allowed the enemy to have. Replace them with the truth of who You are and who we are in You. In Jesus' name, amen.

Chapter 4

The Impact on Our Lives

A Facebook message came from a beautiful young woman who is impacting others for God through her ministry: "Do you ever feel nervous about public speaking? What has kept you moving forward? Are there times when you have felt like hiding from everyone? Have you ever felt so unworthy in ministry that you just want to throw in the towel? I've been feeling this way a lot, and I'm just reaching out for help and maybe encouragement on the journey."

My answer? Yes, been there, felt that.

I wrote back the following:

Yes, I do get nervous sometimes. I recognize that it's usually because I'm either looking at myself or thinking too much about the people who I'm going to speak to and how they will react or what they will think about me. So I start praying and refocusing on God. Reminding myself that it's not about what anyone else thinks. It's about being faithful to what God has called me to do. How people respond, what happens, what anyone thinks, etc., is His job, not mine. . . .

The unworthy part is a different thing. Yes. There are moments—moments when I've wanted to quit and walk away and do something that didn't require me to be up front or where people could see me. Times I've struggled and wanted God to take away my ability to literally speak because I said the wrong things, shared things I shouldn't have, hurt people. I know I'm a sinner. . . .

Thing is, when God reveals to us our not enoughness or sinfulness, it's always a conviction that leads to repentance and greater dependence on Him. It never disqualifies us. When the enemy reminds us of our not enoughness and sinfulness, he condemns us, and we feel guilt, shame, and unworthiness. That's when we want to quit. Truth is, we're not enough. We're not worthy. Never will be. Truth also is, God knows that and He is enough. He calls us anyway. Uses us even when we're broken and empty. I've had my moments where I needed to go and speak and felt so broken, like I had nothing to offer at all—like I was barely hanging on myself. But I had said yes and tickets were bought. God always shows up. Because it's not about what we can do—it's about what He can do. We don't have to be perfect. Just willing to show up.

Willing to tell Him honestly where we're at. Take it to Him. Let Him speak into our lives.

We can't let the enemy win. He longs to devour us and take us out and keep us from doing and being who God created us to be. Sometimes his attack is the greatest just before God is going to use us in a big way or call us to the next step in His plan. The enemy wants to thwart that. So watch for God. He delights in you. . . . He is using you—in ways you may never see this side of eternity.

The enemy wants to keep us from living the life God has planned for us. He doesn't want us to believe what God says about us. He wants to keep us from doing what God has created us to do. So he uses our feelings of not being enough or being too much to cause us to want to quit, avoid trying, say no, and hide away.

We're missing out

I recently created a nonscientific survey that was answered by one hundred women. One question asked was, "Has your not enoughness ever caused you to do any of the following?" with several options. The responses weren't surprising.

- Sixty-four percent of the women said that they had skipped a social event because they didn't feel like they were enough.
- Twenty-six percent didn't talk to someone new because their feelings of not being enough made them think that person would never want to be friends with someone like them.
- Thirty-eight percent of the women said no to a new opportunity, even though they wanted to do it, because they felt they weren't enough.
- When asked, "What do you do when you feel like you're not enough?" 26 percent said they try harder to be enough, while 22 percent said they give up and hide.

My friends, we are missing out on important events in our lives because the enemy has convinced us that we're not enough! We cannot let him win like that.

It's not just jobs, promotions, and social events we're missing out on. Often our fear of not being enough causes us to avoid taking risks and trying new things. It keeps us from connecting with new people and causes us to believe we have to settle instead of waiting for what we really want.

I'm not sure why I remember so clearly the time when I was about seventeen years old and my church took our youth group to a winter camp in New York. There was a small hill that had been made into a ski slope, and all of my friends were trying to "ski" for the first time—except me. I didn't try it because I was afraid I wouldn't be able to do it well and would fall down and look silly. The crazy thing is, most of the teens giving it a shot *were* falling down and looking goofy, but that seemed to make it more fun for them. Yet I couldn't get myself to strap on the skis and hold on to the towrope.

It's not the only time I've missed out on fun because I was afraid of doing something badly, so I didn't even attempt it. And it's not just fun stuff that I've said no to. There have been opportunities to make an impact or to try something I've always wanted to do. But my fear of not being able to do it well caused me to say no.

I regret the missed opportunities. I know I'm not alone. How many of us have let feelings of not being enough or the fear that we couldn't do something well cause us to avoid risks and not pursue a dream or things we long to try? These can be simple things, such as learning to play the piano, giving painting a try, or starting a book club and inviting a few girlfriends. It breaks my heart that the enemy all too often wins the battle over pursuing our dreams and living the lives God created us to live, the lives gifted to us, because God planted the seeds of desire or passion that cause us to want to go after these dreams.

Dream for a moment. If you could do anything and knew you couldn't fail, what would you do?

Did you take a minute to dream or just skip to the next line? Come on, really think about it. Dream a little. What has your heart always dreamed about doing? It doesn't have to be a big career type of dream. Maybe you always wished you could go somewhere or learn something new: a creative-cooking class, start a blog, run a 5K, or write a book.

I've known since I was a little girl that I wanted to be a writer. When our youngest son began school and my husband encouraged me to take time to try pursuing my dream, it was scary and exciting. That first manuscript was rejected. But the editor who read it encouraged me that the idea was good. The writing just needed improvements. She gave me a few ideas. I rewrote it and sent it to another publisher. They read it and decided that it was an idea they wanted to publish, but it needed some more tweaking. I rewrote it again, and *How to Hug a Heart* hit shelves. Yet all of these years and books later, when I sit down to write, I am tempted to fear that no one will be interested in the manuscript; that it will be published, but no one will want to read it; or that it won't be meaningful. I push through those fears because I believe God has called me to write and has put each topic on my heart. I'm willing to take a risk because I'm trusting Him and not myself.

Remember the last chapter when we talked about the enemy attempting to keep us from doing what God has created us to do? He knows that as women, we may not try if we believe we can't do something well or perfectly. So he speaks doubt, fear, and excuses into our thoughts to tempt us to believe we're not enough and cause us to avoid taking risks or try. We have to resist his tempting thoughts and lean on God for courage.

If we won't take risks and try the small things, like skiing or painting or running a 5K or talking to someone new, where will we get the courage to try something big? A new job, writing a book, starting a ministry, or inviting others to serve the community with you in a way that you're passionate about.

Even when we do attempt something new, if we fail or don't do it perfectly the first time, we all too often beat ourselves up and quit. Where did we get the idea that we can't fail or that failure means we should quit? Why do we believe we need to do something perfectly in order to do it? Failure and mistakes are opportunities to learn and grow—learn what doesn't work and try again in a different way. I don't know about you, but I've learned some of the most impacting life lessons through failures and then trying again; I learn more from these failures than from first-time successes. It's not just the opportunities that we're missing but the lessons from trying, failing, and trying again.

Did you know that both Babe Ruth and Hank Aaron had more strikeouts in their careers than home runs? Babe Ruth struck out 1,330 times and had 714 home runs. Aaron struck out 1,383 times and had 755 home runs. Are they remembered for their strikeouts? No, they are remembered as two of the greatest baseball players of all time. Failure, making mistakes, or striking out at whatever we do isn't the end of the world unless we quit, give up, or don't try at all.

We settle for less

"Looking back now, I see how crazy it sounds," shares Emily, who has been married for more than forty years. "I married Bob because he was the first guy who showed an interest, and I thought no one else ever would. This was my only chance. And hey, he was a good-looking, smart, successful man. It was pretty amazing that he would be interested in someone like me. Our relationship wasn't easy. He was always critical of me, pointing out my flaws and mistakes, telling me that he'd help me improve and be a better person. I knew I was a mess and was thankful that while he saw it, too, he was still interested. So when he proposed, I said yes."

Emily sighs sadly. "If I knew then what I know now, I would have made different choices. I would have waited for a man who loved me, who made me feel loved, who saw my flaws and mistakes but encouraged and cheered me on. Bob never did that. Affirming words and encouragement are not his gift. I know he loves me to the best of his ability, and I love him. But it's hard. We don't share the same interests or even some of the same values. I long to have conversations about God and books I'm reading. I wish he valued family and relationships more so we could enjoy more time together with our kids and grandkids. If I could give advice to young women, I'd tell them not to settle, to hold out for a guy who not only loves them but makes them feel loved and cherished. A man who they can be themselves with instead of always fearing what's going to be the next thing he'll be unhappy about."

My heart still hurts as I think about another young woman who had so much going for her. She had a mom and stepdad who loved her and supported her. She was an Olympic-level athlete, completing a college degree in a field she loved. She had recently begun dating a handsome young man who treated her better than any guy ever had. Why then did she give it all up to go back to a previous boyfriend who physically and verbally abused her, cutting her off from the family and friends who loved her? Because she believed the words he taunted her with: "I knew you'd be back; this is all you deserve."

When we don't believe in ourselves or the value God has given us, we often settle for less than what God desires for us and sometimes think we don't deserve anything better. Relationships are a big area where women settle, but they aren't the only ways we settle. We settle and don't expect more in our jobs or careers. We settle and don't expect more from ourselves—more courage, more joy, and more perseverance.

Sometimes the settling is small and seemingly insignificant. I remember stopping at a bakery when craving peanut butter–blossom cookies, which are peanut butter cookies with a chocolate kiss. The shelves were filled with all kinds of cookies but not peanut butter–blossom cookies. I picked up a tray of cookies to share at the office, thinking they'd do, even though they weren't what I wanted. At the checkout counter, the cashier asked whether I had found everything I wanted. I admitted I hadn't. She immediately told me she thought they had just been baking the very cookies I wanted and would be glad to get me a tray fresh from the oven. They would just need to figure out how to package them since the chocolate kisses weren't firm yet. I thanked her but told her not to go to the trouble and took my not-quite-what-I-wanted cookies and left.

Eating my good-enough cookie, it suddenly struck me that I could have had what I was craving, but I said no to the generous offer to pack up warm cookies fresh from the oven. Crazy!

But how often do we say, "No, thank you," when others offer to do something for us or give us something we would enjoy? How many times have we missed out on a blessing because we didn't want to bother someone or didn't want anyone to go to any extra trouble for us? Yet often those of us who say, "No, thank you," the most are the first to offer and truly want to do something for others!

How many times does God attempt to bless us with something our hearts desire, and we miss out because we haven't learned to accept gifts graciously or feel that we are worth the effort? When we settle, we miss out on the good things God has for us.

It's not just us

We're not the only ones missing out. All too often, when we feel like we're not enough or don't measure up, we don't risk trying to make new friendships. Have you ever met someone and thought, *She seems like someone who would be fun to hang out with*? Or have you seen someone at church, enjoyed her insights in a small group, admired the way she did things, and thought she'd be someone you'd like to get to know? Maybe there's a person at work or school who seems to enjoy similar interests, and you've thought about talking to her. But you don't. Maybe you "friend" her on Facebook, but you don't invite her to lunch. "She's probably too busy," you tell yourself.

Many years ago—more than I care to count—I was attending a women's retreat where Ginny Allen was speaking. It was the first of several times I would hear Ginny, who is one of my favorite retreat speakers. Our team had invited a speaker who was unable to attend at the last minute and sent Ginny in her place. Friday evening worship began, and she hadn't arrived. Pittsburgh traffic can be crazy, especially on Friday afternoon. Our team was praying in a back room when Ginny and her joyful spirit came through the door. We knew instantly that God was about to do something big.

Throughout the weekend, Ginny's stories and lessons impacted my heart. I wanted to tell her, but my fear kept me from going up and talking to her. Why would she, a speaker, want to hear from insignificant me? But I began praying and asking God for an opportunity to tell her how He was using her in my life. On Sunday morning, I was up early to spend time with God. My roommate was not a morning person, so I quietly crept into the bathroom and closed the door, finding an uncomfortable spot to sit, study, and pray. Then a crazy thought popped into my head, *Go out and sit on the comfy sofa in the lobby.*

Our room was in a lodge. Just outside our door was a cozy setting of sofas and chairs, which was a much better place to sit and hang out with God than the bathroom. But I refused to go. "I can't let anyone see me looking like this!" I told myself. "Bed head and thick glasses—not a pretty sight." The impression to go out to the sofa was persistent, but I was more persistent in my unwillingness. It couldn't be God, right?

That morning I was sitting on the front row for Ginny's last presentation when she said, "Early this morning, around five A.M., I was sitting on the sofa outside my room, feeling discouraged. I asked God to encourage me."

Suddenly, my mind clicked. I had helped with lodging assignments. I knew Ginny's room was just across the hall from mine. She had been sitting on the sofa, praying for encouragement at the same time I was sitting in the bathroom, refusing the "crazy" thought to go out to the sofa for my quiet time.

"And God sent someone who spoke words of encouragement," she continued.

That was supposed to be me! I realized. God had attempted to answer my prayers for an opportunity to talk to Ginny and tell her how God was using her—words that would have encouraged her—and I had let the fear of what someone might think about how I look at five in the morning keep me from doing it.

I remember the story clearly all of these years later because God used it to convict me and remind me that people are people. Those we deem important need encouragement and friends just as much as we do. And all too often people shy away from them, thinking they wouldn't need another friend or are too busy or too important. I determined that morning not to let my fears and doubts about myself and my enoughness get in the way of encouraging others. I may need to send up a prayer for courage, but I take a deep breath and reach out, attempt to connect, and speak words of encouragement.

My friend, God has placed people in your path that He knows you can impact in simple yet life-changing ways. Your sense of humor, gift of encouragement, life lessons, or invitation to participate in something will be just the thing they need. A card, a home-cooked meal, or a playdate for your kids—there are so many simple ways we can connect with others and build friendships if we're willing to try.

Missing opportunities to impact

As the young woman I mentioned at the beginning of this chapter and I talked, she asked whether she could share my messages with a friend, who was another talented young woman who told her that she had sat in the pew for years because she never felt good enough or worthy enough to be up front and use her gifts to serve God. This is an area where the enemy loves to attack. He longs for us to feel unworthy to serve God and question our ability to minister to others. He will tempt us to think, *Someone else can do it better; I'm not a good Christian, so I shouldn't be doing this.*

When God was first calling me to serve His daughters, the church I was attending asked me to serve as their head deaconess. Women's ministry was only just beginning, and most churches hadn't added it to their ministry list. I was excited about the possibilities of using this leadership role to create opportunities for women to get together, study together, and encourage one another.

Then I heard that one of the older women in the church was telling people I should not be the head deaconess because I wasn't a good example of a Christian woman and was not a submissive wife. My friends laughed when they told me because they thought I was too submissive as a wife. And they knew my heart— how much I loved God and took serving Him seriously. They didn't realize how the enemy would use these words to attempt to take out my heart by making me wonder whether they were true. (Why did I believe words spoken by someone who didn't know me, instead of my friends?)

I was in tears when I told my husband that I was going to turn down the opportunity. His words made me stop crying and start praying and asking God for wisdom. "Tami, you felt God calling you to this. You've been excited about it. Don't let the enemy win."

After praying and fasting for a week, I said yes.

A year later, when the woman who had spoken the words that had devastated my heart moved, she came to me and said, "Keep doing what you're doing. God is using you. You are a great mom and are doing good work."

I had almost let the enemy keep me from doing something God had called me to do because someone's words had hurt me and caused me to believe I wasn't good enough to serve. The challenge from my husband, a lot of prayers, a great team, and a year of serving God's women at our church had changed not only me but also the woman who had spoken words over a person she didn't even know.

How often we let words, experiences, or opinions keep us from doing what God has called us to do. We allow our feelings of not being enough or being unworthy to get in the way of using our gifts to serve. We sit in the pew, thinking everyone else has their lives more together. We hesitate to share our thoughts and insights in Bible studies and small groups. We don't share our ideas because we believe that no one would be interested.

When we let our not enoughness keep us from using our gifts and passions, from reaching out to people God has placed in our paths, and from waiting for what God desires instead of settling, we're not living the life God planned. We're letting the enemy win.

Our focus

Sadly, without even realizing it, we are too often focused on ourselves and all we're not, instead of trying, risking, pursuing dreams and relationships, or experiencing all that God has planned for us. The problem isn't our not enoughness; the problem is our focus.

We need to stop seeing all we're not and look to God and all He is and has promised. It sounds easy—stop thinking about yourself and think about God and others—but it can be hard to live out. Remember, we have this enemy who is persistently seeking to steal, kill, destroy, and devour. So, while we try to focus on God and not ourselves, the enemy will constantly look for opportunities to remind us of our not enoughness. And he's right; we're not enough. But that doesn't disqualify us from doing what God called us to do because God is enough to work in and through us to accomplish what He desires. And when He does, it changes us. It gives us more courage. It makes us stronger. God can do amazing things through us, even when we're struggling and don't believe in ourselves, if we just trust Him. Remember what I told the young woman?

God always shows up. Because it's not about what we can do—it's about what He can do. We don't have to be perfect. Just willing to show up. Willing to tell Him honestly where we're at. Take it to Him. Let Him speak into our lives.

We can't let the enemy win. He longs to devour us and take us out and keep us from doing and being who God created us to be. Sometimes his attack is the greatest just before God is going to use us in a big way or call us to the next step in His plan. The enemy wants to thwart that. So watch for God. He delights in you. . . . He is using you—in ways you may never see this side of eternity.

Your story
- Are there things you haven't attempted to do because you didn't think you could do them well?
- Who have you missed out connecting with and possibly building a friendship with because you didn't think they would want to hang out with someone like you?

- What has God called you to do that you've been unwilling to try because you didn't think you could do it well enough?
- Are there areas of your life where you have settled instead of pursuing, waiting for, or believing God had something more?
- How would you like to serve God? What are your gifts and talents? Are you using them? If not, why not?

God is enough
God is enough to give you the courage to risk and try, pick you back up when you fail, and cheer you on as you press through the fears and doubts.

Promise
"I can do all things through Christ who strengthens me" (Philippians 4:13).

Prayer
O Father God, Provider, the One who formed us before we were born and calls us by name, how You love us! How You never give up on us! Please forgive us for the ways we've believed the enemy and settled for less than what You've promised or called us to. Reveal to us the things we're believing and the way we're letting it get in the way of the life You've planned for us. Father, forgive us for giving up, quitting, not trying, and failing to believe Your promises about Your plans for us—good plans filled with hope for our future. Give us the courage to forgive ourselves, believe You have more for us than we often expect, and live for You, using our gifts and passions to serve You, reaching out to others and encouraging them in the journey. We love You, Lord. In Jesus' name, amen.

Chapter 5

The Impact on Our Relationships

She wanted to be in the living room, listening to the stories and hearing the lessons. Jesus taught with an authority that she had never heard before. She had invited Him into her home because she wanted to hear more and get to know this Man and His teachings (Luke 10:38).

But she knew that she didn't deserve to be in the living room. She was a woman. Martha lived in a time when women were not to be seen or heard. She would make her very best meal, serve with great efficiency, and make sure that she impressed Jesus—all in order to prove that she was enough to be His friend.

As Martha carried a bowl of steaming lentils to the table where the men were gathered, she caught sight of someone who didn't belong: Mary! She was sitting in the living room with the men, listening; her eyes were focused intently on Jesus. Not fair! Mary should be helping her, not getting to listen. Martha wanted to listen too. She had sat at His feet and heard Him teach and wanted more, but she now sought to impress Him and get His attention by her service. And Mary should be helping too. She tried quietly to get Mary's attention and motioned for her to help, but Mary never looked in her direction.

Martha fumed to herself as she went back to the kitchen for more food. She placed the plate of fresh-baked bread, still warm and fragrant from the oven, on the table in front of the men a little harder than necessary when she returned. Peter looked her way, then quickly turned his attention back to Jesus, but Mary didn't budge. "It's not fair!" Martha told herself as she made another trip to her kitchen. "I always get stuck doing the work, while she does whatever she wants. Everyone pays attention to her and wants to talk with her, but they just want me for what I can do to serve. Even Jesus doesn't care!"

Returning once again with a bowl of fresh fruit, Martha couldn't take it any longer. Slamming the bowl on the table so hard that everyone, including Jesus, stopped and looked at her, she demanded, "Do You not care that my sister has left me to serve alone? Therefore tell her to help me" (verse 40).

It's an age-old story. Think Rachel and Leah: sisters competing for the attention and love of one man; Sarah and Hagar: a beautiful, rich woman jealous of her servant; Hannah and Peninnah: one having her husband's love but longing for babies, and the other having babies and longing for her husband's love.

Women compare and compete. We do it without even intentionally thinking about it. How many times have we entered a room full of women and instantly started looking at what they were wearing, how they looked, those who were gathered around talking and laughing with them, and compared ourselves? Sometimes we feel better—thinner, prettier, or dressed trendier. But all too often, we feel less than—not as pretty, thin, or stylish. We do it at work and school. Someone compliments a woman, and we instantly feel like we are not enough, and we don't measure up because we can't do what she does or do it as well as she does.

Comparing our lives to others turns into competing with them without even thinking about it. We're encouraged to compete. Women's magazines love to run articles on who wore a dress better. Somehow one woman's success minimizes what we've achieved or are doing.

Social media has created a whole new level of comparing and competing. At any time, day or night, we can scroll through our feed and see the Instagram-filtered pictures of other people's lives, while forgetting that they may have gone through a dozen photos before finding one they were willing to post and that one only after applying a filter. Pictures of vacations and outings with friends make us feel boring and friendless, uninvited, less than, and not enough. We don't consider that sometimes the fun photos don't tell the whole story of struggling marriages, loneliness despite the activities, and insecurities that are longing for more likes and comments.

The trouble with comparing and competing is that it prevents us from caring and connecting. You can't really care about someone with whom you're competing. And you're not seeing their whole lives or who they really are if you're viewing them through their Instagram feed and the filter of your insecurities. All too often, when we compare and compete and don't measure up, we give up. We don't try. We stay busy in the kitchen instead of reaching out in friendship. We can't truly love, encourage, and be there for someone whom we feel less than or are trying to beat.

Danger of the not-enough filter

"She must be mad at me," I told my husband as we drove home from church. "She didn't talk to me at all today. Didn't even look at me. I don't know what I did."

Now I do. I had jumped to conclusions. My friend had been aloof that morning at church. I had tried to talk to her, but she didn't seem interested in a conversation. She kept busy with her kids. I instantly wondered what I did wrong. How sad that when we believe we're not enough, if something isn't right, we often instantly assume that we must have done something wrong. I'm not alone in this, am I? You get called into the boss's office, and as you head that direction, you wonder what you did wrong. Your husband is grouchy and focused on football, and you take it personally. A friend doesn't call you back, and you think she must be mad about something. Someone is great at something, and you assume she wouldn't be interested in a friendship with you because you're not good at anything.

I later found out that my friend was struggling with a mistake she had made at work. She was beating herself up over it and had just felt so bad that she didn't want to talk to anyone. It wasn't about me. It was about her battle. But because I assumed that I had done something wrong and hadn't considered that she was struggling, I didn't push through her aloofness and find a way to encourage her.

The assumptions we make about people, filtered through our perspective of not being enough, sometimes cause us to disregard that they could be struggling and need a friend. Instead, we beat ourselves up for something we didn't do. Martha's real struggle wasn't with Mary's failure to help; it was with her own feeling of not being enough and trying to prove herself to Jesus. Her resulting jealousy was because Mary was doing the very thing Martha wanted to do.

I constantly remind myself to consider the other person's possible perspective when the enemy tempts me to think it's about me. Could he or she be struggling? Maybe this person needs encouragement or a friend? How can I respond, or what can I do if it's not about me?

I was attempting to build a friendship with a beautiful and intelligent woman I'll call Cara. It was hard because I was getting mixed signals. Cara would be friendly and do something kind for me one week. Then she would be distant and aloof the next. Sometimes it even felt like she wanted to pick a fight with me. I fought the enemy's temptation to believe that this was about me and not being enough for Cara to want to be friends. I thought through our friendship and time together and couldn't think of any reason that she'd treat me this way. So I prayed and stepped out in the belief that there was something Cara was struggling with personally. I resisted the temptation to retreat and instead looked for ways to encourage and affirm her. She seemed surprised by my affirmations. I persisted. Eventually, she shared that she'd been hurt by a friend who was constantly critical of her and whose comments made her feel like she just wasn't enough. The experience had obviously left her a little leery of friendships.

There are a lot of wounded women walking around. We are wounded by friends, parents, husbands, or coworkers. Our wounds can make us a bit gun-shy around each other and cause us to avoid building friendships for fear that we'll be hurt again.

I remember going through a time when several friendships seemed to end in hurtful ways, one right after another. I decided that I didn't want to try again. I'd be nice to people and encourage others when I had the chance, but I wasn't going to attempt close friendships again. That didn't last long, and God brought a beautiful new friend into my life whose deep commitment to Him continues to inspire and challenge me.

Barriers or bridges?

The enemy doesn't want us connecting and caring about each other, so he uses our belief that we're not enough to create barriers instead of building bridges. He allows wounds from our previous relationships to keep us from being willing to connect past the surface and past the superficial conversations we have all too often:

"Hi, how are you?"

"I'm fine. How are you?"

"I'm fine."

The thing is, we're not always fine. We're lying because we believe others won't care; it's not safe to be honest; or we should be perfect, so we don't let anyone think that we're not. (And it's not always safe or a good idea to tell our stories to everyone who asks how we're doing, but we need to have people in our lives with whom we can be honest about our struggles.)

I really believe that if we could be more honest with each other about where we're at and how we're struggling, we'd connect with each other and encourage each other more.

"I was surprised that Jennifer admitted she struggles with the leftover cheesecake in the refrigerator," Glenna said one day after Bible study. Glenna was a new Christian—or trying to decide whether she wanted to be a Christian. She wasn't sure she was good enough. She'd lived a tough life. "I didn't think Christian women struggled with the same things I do."

She paused and was thoughtful. "But it really surprised me when a couple of women talked about struggling in their marriages. I thought Christian wives never got mad at their husbands and just—I don't know—lived that 'happily ever after' life you read about."

The women in our small group shared honestly about their struggles. It bonded our group and gave Glenna courage and the hope that maybe she wasn't so bad after all. A few months later, Glenna committed her life to Christ and was baptized.

It's not just our girlfriends

"Why won't she believe me?" one husband asked. He was frustrated because no matter how often he told his wife that she was beautiful, she didn't believe him. She continued to beat herself up for not being thin enough, for the wrinkles beginning to appear on her face, for the grays that were popping up faster and faster, and too often standing frustrated in her closet, not knowing what to wear because she felt nothing looked good on her.

"I really do think she looks beautiful. She's kind and caring. Generous. I just wish she would believe me." He sounded sad and frustrated. He loved her. He believed in her, and he wanted her to see it.

All too often, our battle with feeling like we are not enough impacts the guys in our lives who are trying to love us well. I know some of you who are reading this don't have men who are loving you well. They subtract from your view of yourself with their hurtful words and critical attitudes. If you're in a relationship with someone who treats you like that, talk to a trusted Christian counselor. If you're dating, pray and ask God whether this is what He wants for you and the way He wants you to be treated. Don't settle because you think you're not worth someone treating you better. You are. If you're married, work with a Christian counselor on ways to handle the situation and don't allow it to define you. Remember that God wants you to value yourself by the price He paid for you. It was costly, but He has never regretted it. He loves you so very much.

Some of us do have men who are attempting to do their best to encourage us, compliment us, and tell us we did a great job. They want us to believe them and value their comments. How do we dismiss their attempts to affirm us?

He says, "You look great in that dress!"

"This old thing? You've seen me in it before." Without thinking about it, you've diminished his compliment.

"You're going to do a great job with your presentation at work today. They're going to be glad they hired you," he encourages as you get ready for work and an important meeting.

"I doubt that it will even make a difference. I'm sure they're going to go with the proposal Dan brings instead. I just don't have enough experience to know what they want yet," you sigh as you deflect his encouragement and let your belief that you're not enough take over your thinking.

Eventually, most men give up. They battle too. They want to be successful, and if they can't succeed in encouraging us, they just stop. They think, *She's not going to believe me anyway.* And then we're hurt that our husbands don't speak words of encouragement, never realizing how often they've tried and we've refused to believe them.

Can I encourage you to do something here? Next time your guy compliments you, simply say, "Thank you." Let him know that you appreciate his encouraging words. Roll them around in your head. Repeat them to yourself. Give yourself permission to believe him instead of the enemy. Your guy loves you. The enemy hates you. Who do you want to believe?

I admit that I often dismissed my husband when he told me I was beautiful. Sometimes when he tells me now, and I say, "Thank you," he looks at me and says, "You don't really believe me." I laugh. He's right. I don't think I'm beautiful. But I *do* think and like that *he* thinks I'm beautiful.

We don't intentionally diminish or disbelieve our husbands' (or anyone's) compliments or attempts to affirm and encourage us. Most of us *want* encouragement and affirmation. We just don't know what to do with it. We feel awkward. Sometimes we think they're just being nice or they "have" to say nice things because they're our husbands. My sons often said moms always compliment you, believe in you, and affirm you. My oldest once said, "Moms love you no matter what, even if you're an ax murderer." This thinking made it easy for them to dismiss the words I spoke over their lives. But you and I know that not all moms speak words of affirmation or belief nor do all husbands or friends. We need to give ourselves permission to receive others' words graciously, even if it's just to simply say, "Thank you!" We also need to give ourselves permission to ponder the words. Hold on to them. Believe that there's something true in them about who we are and how others see us. Girlfriend, you are more beautiful—inside and out—than you believe you are! Trust the people who love you most and not the one who hates you and is out to destroy you.

Others in the room

A word of warning: others are listening and watching how we respond and how we talk about ourselves. They're listening to how we accept or condemn compliments and affirmation. They're listening to what we're saying through our words about ourselves and our actions to learn what it means to be a woman.

Who are these people? Our daughters.

We can compliment and encourage them all we want and tell them they're smart, talented, creative, beautiful, caring, and kind. But if they hear us continually putting ourselves down, dismissing compliments, and disbelieving that we have much to offer the world around us, they'll grow up thinking that's how women talk about themselves.

Ladies, we need to learn to live the way we want our daughters to live. If we want them to believe in themselves, then we need to model this belief. If we want them to believe that a woman is more than a dress size or number on a scale, then we need to live like that's true. If we want them to pursue their dreams, attempt to achieve their goals, and learn to try and fail and try again, then we need to set the example. If we want them to pursue God's will for their lives, we need to learn not to settle in ours. If we don't want them beating themselves up and talking negatively about who they are, then we need to show them how to be positive.

We need to remind our daughters of who they are in Christ and all that He's promised them and then live like we believe this is true for us too.

How we see God

Did you notice what Martha asked first when she approached Jesus and demanded that He tell Mary to get up and help her? "Lord, do You not care that my sister has left me to serve alone?" (Luke 10:40).

God, don't You care?

At that moment, she felt like life wasn't fair. She was working hard and trying to do what she thought everyone expected and wanted from her. She was trying to prove herself and impress Jesus. But He didn't even seem to notice. No one seemed to notice. Her hard work wasn't getting her anywhere except frustrated, tired, and angry. She definitely didn't feel loved. And Jesus just sat there, letting it all happen. He must not care!

How often, when we feel like we're not enough or are too much, do we try to fix ourselves on our own? Do more. Try harder. Try to make people like us and accept us. Seek affirmation. Prove ourselves and our worth. And when nothing works out the way we thought it should, we wonder where God is and whether He truly cares. How can He accept us when we don't accept ourselves?

The enemy loves to cause us to doubt God's love and care or see God as judging, demanding, and punishing. Our not enoughness can cause us to doubt we're good enough for God to love or use. We may think He wishes we would get it right, which causes us to wonder whether He can forgive us again, pushing us to do more and try harder to make ourselves worthy of His love.

Yes, we sing, "Jesus loves me, this I know," and we believe it—sort of. We believe it in our heads but not at the core of who we are. We don't live from this belief that God loves us. John did. When he wrote about Jesus, he identified himself as the "disciple whom Jesus loved" (John 21:7; cf. 13:23; 19:26; 20:2; 21:20). Jesus loved all of His disciples, not just John. Yet for John, Christ's love was what gave him his identity and purpose. It changed how he viewed himself and his life. It motivated all he did and how he saw God.

This is how we need to live: believing in God's love for us, uniquely and individually, at the core of who we are and letting that change how we see ourselves, interact with others, and live our lives. Believing in God's love shifts our focus to Him and His love instead of on ourselves and our not enoughness. Stop trying to be enough, and let God be enough.

What did Martha do?

Martha's story in Luke 10 closes with Jesus' famous words, which are all too often read as a rebuke. I don't think Jesus was verbally beating her up. I believe His words were inviting her to discover that He was enough: "Martha, Martha, you are worried and troubled about many things. But one thing is needed, and Mary has chosen that good part, which will not be taken away from her" (verses 41, 42).

"Martha, Martha." Jesus repeats her name to ensure that she's paying attention and snap her away from her frustrations and anger to focus on Him and His words. Picture Him saying her name gently, lovingly, inviting her to learn something new that would change everything.

"You are worried and troubled about many things." He sees her. He knows her heart. He knows that she's focused on the meal, serving well, and impressing Him, and it's causing her heart to ache and fear that she's not enough. He *sees* her.

"But one thing is needed." One thing was needed—*needed*. And it wasn't a list of things Martha should accomplish or do. How often do we approach our relationship with God using the word *should* instead of *need*? I should spend more time with God. I should study my Bible. I should pray more. I should get involved in something at church. I *should* . . . The trouble is that *should* isn't a great motivator. We know we should exercise, but it doesn't get us up and out of bed and to the gym. We know we should eat healthily, but that doesn't stop us from going through the drive-through when we're in a rush and are hungry. *Should* won't grow our relationship with God. *Need* is different. When we need something, we do it. We

recognize the true importance of it. Mary knew she needed time with God—*needed* Him. She couldn't live life without Him.

"Mary has chosen that good part." It's a choice. Mary chose to sit and listen. She made a relationship with Him more important than anything, even going against her world's rule that women shouldn't be in the room listening to men talk. She even risked making her sister mad. (She knew that Martha would have a fit if she didn't help. Siblings know what push each other's buttons.)

"Which will not be taken away from her." The time we spend with Jesus speaks into our lives. The verses we memorize are stored in our brains, available for when the Holy Spirit knows we need to be reminded. The songs we sing repeat in our thinking, often popping into our thoughts just when we need a song. The lessons we learn impact and change our lives. So much of what we do is undone almost as soon as we finish it:

- cleaning the house
- doing laundry
- making a meal
- giving a report at school
- teaching a fourth-grader a list of spelling words

But time spent with God lasts.

How does Martha respond to Jesus' invitation?

There is no verse 43 in Luke 10. To see how this conversation affected Martha, we need to turn to John 11 and pick up Martha's story. Lazarus, her brother, is sick and dying. He is the head of their home. It's Lazarus, Mary, and Martha. Life will be hard in many ways if he dies. But they know Jesus can heal him. They've seen Him heal others and even heard stories of Him raising people from the dead. So they send a messenger to tell Him what's happening. The message is simple: "Lord, behold, he whom You love is sick" (verse 3).

Note the new Martha. She doesn't doubt God's love. She doesn't tell Him what to do. She trusts and believes that because He loves Lazarus, He'll do the right thing.

John continues the story. "When Jesus heard that, He said, 'This sickness is not unto death, but for the glory of God, that the Son of God may be glorified' " (verse 4).

Then John inserts a little statement before telling us the next part of the story: "Now Jesus loved Martha and her sister and Lazarus" (verse 5). John wants to remind readers that Jesus loved this family. And then he goes on with the story. "So, when He heard that he was sick, He stayed two more days in the place where He was" (verse 6). Jesus loves them, but He doesn't go. He stays put. How will it feel to hear the report from the messenger repeating these words and then watch Lazarus die?

When Jesus finally arrives, Lazarus has been dead for four days. The belief at the time said that the spirit lingered for three days, but by the fourth, all hope was gone. That's when Jesus shows up. Well, actually He never got a chance to get there. As soon as Martha hears He's coming, she leaves those gathered at their home to grieve and rushes to Jesus. She's changed. No longer trying to impress or measure up to what's expected, she runs to Jesus.

"Now Martha said to Jesus, 'Lord, if You had been here, my brother would not have died. But even now I know that whatever You ask of God, God will give You' " (verses 21, 22). At first glance, we may think that Martha is asking Jesus to raise Lazarus from the dead. But even after this conversation, when Jesus tells some people to roll away the stone, Martha is the one who attempts to stop Him because of the smell and her desire to respect Lazarus. She never expects Jesus to raise her brother. So what do her words mean?

"But even now I know . . ." These are incredible, faith-filled words. Even now, I know that despite the fact You didn't come when I needed You most; even now, when I don't know how Mary and I will manage without a man in our home—even now, I believe that whatever You ask God, He does. She goes on to proclaim, "I believe that You are the Christ, the Son of God, who is to come into the world" (verse 27).

Martha has discovered that Jesus is enough, even when life is incredibly hard.

This "enoughness" in Jesus changes how she sees Mary. No longer comparing and competing, she knows that Mary needs Jesus at this moment. She runs back to their home and tells Mary, "The Teacher has come and is calling for you" (verse 28). Such a beautiful act of kindness! She knows Mary is hurting, struggling, and wondering why this happened. Mary repeats Martha's words: "Lord, if You had been here, my brother would not have died" (verse 32). But she does not go on to speak trust and belief in this hard moment. Martha knows her sister needs Jesus. She needs to see Him and trust Him.

Friends, the enemy will attempt to use our fears, doubts, and shame that we're not enough to disconnect us from others. He will try to make us compare ourselves with other women in ways that either drive us to compete with them or make us shy away and hide, so we won't reach out and connect. He will tempt us to doubt words of affirmation spoken to us by those we love, using these times as opportunities to discourage others through our diminishment or disbelief. He wants to make sure our young women and girls learn that this is how women talk about themselves.

He is out to steal our joy, kill our friendships, devour our relationships, and destroy our example. But we can stop him and resist him. We can choose the one thing that is needed: an intimate and real relationship with Christ that causes us to believe His love for us, His words about us, and the value He gives us.

Your story

- How have your insecurities or feelings of not measuring up impacted your friendships or possible friendships?

- Could you relate to the idea of comparing and competing? Be aware, and try to catch yourself doing it. Stop. Resist and tell yourself that another person's successes don't diminish yours.
- How good are you at accepting compliments and affirmation? If you're not great at it, start practicing saying, "Thank you," and giving yourself permission to think about these compliments and believe them.
- Have your insecurities and feelings of not being enough impacted your relationship with God? Have you been tempted, like Martha, to try to prove yourself to Him? Or doubt His love?
- What's one thing you can do to choose the one thing needed?

God is enough

God is enough for your relationships. He can love you and delight in you *and* love and delight in others too.

Promise

"Yes, I have loved you with an everlasting love; therefore with lovingkindness I have drawn you" (Jeremiah 31:3).

Prayer

Father God, thank You for loving me, for patiently drawing me closer to You, and for never giving up on me. Thank You that You don't scold or accuse or shame. Thank You for persistently inviting me to something bigger and deeper in You, for pursuing me with Your love, and for wanting more for my friendships, marriage, and daughters. God, help me to choose the one thing that is needed: You. Deepen my understanding of who You are and who I am in You, and grow my trust in You so that I can say, "But even now, when life is hard, I believe." I love You, Lord. Help me to love You more. In Jesus' name, amen.

Part 2

The Lie, the Truth,
and a Big-Enough God

Then Jesus said to those Jews who believed Him, "If you abide in My word, you are My disciples indeed. And you shall know the truth, and the truth shall make you free."

—John 8:31, 32

Discovering the truth about who you are, who God is,
and how He loves you will set you free.

Chapter 6

The Lie

For years, I thought I knew the lie. I watched for it in my life and tried to resist it when I recognized it. I even warned other women about it and told them it wasn't true.

I thought the enemy was lying to us when he tells us we're not enough. He wants us to believe that we're not enough so that we won't live the lives God created us to live and be the unique people He created us to be. He longs to push us to hide; feel shame, self-condemnation, and fear; and become busy with trying harder and harder. This is how and where the enemy wants us to live.

Sometimes he is lying when he tells us we're not enough, even though we really are. He wants to destroy us. He will lie and accuse, shame, and guilt us. We need to watch and resist the temptation to believe that what he says about us is true.

But sometimes he is telling the truth: we're not enough in some areas. Let's face it; no one can be good at everything. Period. I was going to write, "No one can be good at everything all the time." But the truth is, none of us can be good at everything. We just weren't created that way. We were each created with unique gifts and talents. Our brains are wired in certain ways: left brain and right brain. Some of us are good at math and others at telling stories. Some are more athletic and others more into books. Some are great with kids, and others excel at leadership. None of us can do everything perfectly. The enemy will zero in on what we're not good at and cause us to think we should be, and then we criticize and blame ourselves for not measuring up in this area.

Sometimes the enemy attempts to direct our focus on expectations that may or may not be realistic—or even worth striving toward. These expectations can be about how we look or dress; what our success or accomplishments should look like; or what a good mom, wife, friend, daughter, student, worker, or whatever-ideal-you're-trying-to-meet looks like. All too often, these expectations are set by someone who doesn't really know us or love us. Sometimes they are expectations no one can meet. And sometimes they are created by a world that isn't interested in God's expectations.

It usually doesn't matter whether the enemy is lying or telling the truth. We feel our not enoughness and let it drive us toward one of three things: beating ourselves up, hiding, or trying harder. Sometimes we do a combination of all three.

Yet all too often, no matter how hard we try—and we *do* try—we cannot make ourselves enough. We can do a good job, a great job, at many things. But there will always be areas of our lives where we fail and where we don't measure up; we sin, struggle, and battle; or we just weren't created to be good at. Honestly, I can be doing well in most areas of my life and even feel pretty good about myself, but let one person be critical or one negative thought pop in my head, and I begin beating myself up for not being enough. It's as though everyone can cheer me on except for one person in the room, and I'll side with that one person. Or I don't allow myself the grace to fail sometimes or not be good at something.

I'm not alone. We all battle with stuff. We struggle with different things, but we all struggle.

Sophie is successful in her career; she's even been recognized by her peers for the work she does. But she battles feeling not educated enough. She's self-taught, learning most of her skills from experience. She's worked hard to learn and grow and be good at what she does. But everyone on her team except for her has a college education, and it causes her to feel less than and as though she's not enough. Instead of celebrating her accomplishments and the difference she's making at her organization, she beats herself up and often wonders whether she should quit so someone "educated enough" can do her job.

Joy lives up to her name. She radiates joy and beauty. People feel welcome in her presence. She has an innate ability to make people feel comfortable and seen by her interest in them and her invitations that include them in whatever is happening. But sometimes just getting out of the house is hard because she doesn't like how she looks. She beats herself up for the few extra pounds she's put on since turning fifty. She tries to exercise and eat right. And she has good days and bad days. But when she looks in the mirror, she doesn't like what she sees and figures other people are disappointed with her too.

Cameron is a mom to three kids under the age of eight. She fears that she's not enough as a mom. She's sure she's failing her kids somehow. She's exhausted. Her kids are involved in sports and activities every day after school. On weekends, they're busy with groups from church. Then there's juggling homework assignments and getting the kids to bed at a decent time, plus cooking healthy meals and squeezing in family worship at some point. And . . . She just keeps adding to the list of things she should be doing in order to be a good mom, but she feels worse about herself with every added expectation.

We believe we're not enough, and we try harder to improve and make ourselves be enough: be a great mom, impress the boss with our latest project, or measure up to what we think others are doing and achieving. We think it's somehow up to us to make ourselves be enough. But when we don't succeed and feel like we're never going to arrive at being enough, shame and guilt cloak us like a cloud, impacting how we see ourselves, others, and God.

This is when the enemy wins: he convinces us that it's up to us to make ourselves be enough, and he traps us in a cycle of self-condemnation, striving, and shame.

This is important. We need really to understand this. Stop and ponder this idea for a moment: *the real lie isn't that we're not enough; the real lie is that* we *need to make ourselves be enough.*

Friends, God isn't asking us to make ourselves be enough. He wants our not enoughness to drive us to Him. He wants us to bring our battles to Him and talk to Him about who we are and the expectations that drive us. He longs for us to surrender our shame and guilt to Him. He desires that we discover our identity, our value, and our confidence in Him alone—not in trying harder, not in our successes or accomplishments, not in our mirrors or scales, and not in how well we do as wives, moms, friends, daughters, students, or workers.

As with Martha, He invites us to choose Him over striving, trying, beating ourselves up, comparing and competing with others, and giving up. He wants us to rest in Him from the battle and find joy, hope, peace, and abundant life (all things He's promised) instead of living in shame, guilt, hopelessness, and discouragement and with the constant striving to do more or be more.

He's promised that *He* and *His love* will make us whole and holy. "Long before he laid down earth's foundations, he had us in mind, had settled on us as the focus of his love, to be made whole and holy by his love" (Ephesians 1:4, *The Message*).

He's promised that *He* will finish the work in us. "Being confident of this very thing, that He who has begun a good work in you will complete it until the day of Jesus Christ" (Philippians 1:6).

The enemy wants us to feel as though we are not enough so that it drives us to shame and self-condemnation. He wants us to hide from people and opportunities. He wants us to try harder and harder and feel worse about ourselves. I've said it over and over, but we really need to understand what the Bible is telling us and keep reminding ourselves until we live like it's true. The enemy wants to steal, kill, destroy, and devour *you*—and every single one of us.

Don't let this scare, worry, or cause you to feel anxious. Just tell yourself the rest of the story.

God loves you. *He* makes you enough. He *is* working in you. At this very moment, He *is* working to make you whole and holy and draw you to Himself. He loves you with a crazy, head-over-heels, never-going-to-end, bigger-than-any-love-song type of love.

He knows that you're not enough. He wants you to rest in the promise that *He* is enough. God longs for your not enoughness to drive you to Him and the love, joy, hope, peace, and abundant life found in Him alone.

Take it to Him

There's a song on a CD in my car that I often play on repeat when I need a reminder of what God says about me. The lyrics talk about feeling like we are not enough. They compare our feelings to what God says is true about us. There's one part where the song mentions taking all of our failures *and* our successes and laying them at His feet.

This is what God invites us to do:

- Bring our not enoughness (and our enoughness) to Him.
- Tell Him the areas in which you battle.
- Invite Him into these areas of your life.
- Ask Him for healing.
- Give Him your successes.
- Ask Him to remove any pride or any sense that *you* are making yourself be enough.
- Give Him the authority to convict and change you.

Let your not enoughness drive you to Him instead of trying to make yourself more so that He accepts you or can use you to impact others.

He already accepts you. He is already working in and through you. Trust Him. There's no one who knows you better, including all of your great parts and all of your messy parts. He knows and loves you more than anyone ever has or ever will.

We are not our failures. We are not our successes. We are God's daughters. We are forgiven, redeemed, chosen, and delighted in—the apple of His eye. We will fail, but He will redeem. We will struggle, but He will bring peace and joy. We will sometimes feel like we're never going to win the battle, but He says we are more than conquerors. *More than conquerors!*

You are not enough, and God knows this. You don't have to make yourself good enough. You just need to let your not enoughness drive you to discover that God and His love are enough.

Your story

- How has your striving to be enough impacted your heart and the way you see yourself? Has it impacted how you see God? Others?
- What happens in your heart as you begin to understand that *you* don't need to make yourself be enough?
- Does it bring you courage and hope to believe that God is enough for your not enoughness and that He *is* making you enough?
- How can this slight switch in thinking change what you tell yourself when the enemy tries to beat you up?

God is enough

God is enough for your not enoughness or too muchness.

Promise

"The LORD your God in your midst,

The Mighty One, will save;
He will rejoice over you with gladness,
He will quiet you with His love,
He will rejoice over you with singing"
(Zephaniah 3:17).

Prayer

Father God, thank You for being enough! Thank You for knowing every truth about who I am, even the inside stuff no one else sees, yet loving me anyway. Thank You for promising that You will make me whole and holy. Thank You that even now You are working to convict, change, grow, affirm, encourage, and draw me closer to You. Thank You that I can rest in You and find peace, joy, hope, and abundant life. Father, by the authority of Jesus and His sacrifice, remove all the strongholds of the enemy in my thinking and in my heart. Let Your Spirit and Your Word speak truth into those places. Give me the courage to believe Your love and Your work. Keep drawing me deeper. In Jesus' name, amen.

Chapter 7

The Truth

When we believe that we're not enough, it becomes the filter through which we see our world, ourselves, and others. It shapes what we believe people are thinking about us and why they're responding the way they do. It becomes the frame for picturing our abilities and our responses to the opportunities that come our way. It can cause us to look to others for validation or condemnation—giving circumstances and people more power than they should have.

The enemy will use every opportunity he can to repeat the message that we are not enough. But what if we changed our response to his temptation to beat ourselves up for not being enough and turned to God instead? What if we let each thought that we're not enough remind us to depend on God? What if we let each not-enough moment be a time to remember how great God's love is for us? What if we changed our thinking and started believing and constantly reminding ourselves that God is enough? What if we allowed that to be the filter through which we see ourselves?

> Every human being has some vital place in her life where she is not living in the victory she longs for, and it colors how she views herself. Every person's personal struggle rooted in her past, be it a deep-rooted self-hatred or a pressing need to control her world, makes her desperate for God. We all have something that brings us to our knees. It isn't something we would ever choose for ourselves or wish on anyone else, but we all have an area—or ten—in our lives that drives us to need God. We can't free ourselves. We are weak, aware that something inside is broken and starving. It is a wonderful grace when we finally give up and fall down before the One who is strong.[1]

When we fall before God and bring Him our not enoughness, we will discover the truth. God is enough. His Word is filled with promises that He is enough.

- He is enough to forgive and change us when we sin (Romans 5:8; 1 John 1:9).
- He is strong enough when we fail or are weak and messy (2 Corinthians 12:9).

- He promises wisdom when we feel we're not smart enough or we don't have all the answers (James 1:5).
- He chooses specific talents and abilities for each of us to make the impact on the world He desires, even if we fear we don't have what it takes or aren't good at anything (1 Corinthians 12:11).
- He offers a friendship that will never give up on us, never abandon us or betray us, regardless of how others have treated us or how worthy of friendship we deem ourselves (John 15:15).
- He sees our beauty because He designed it, intentionally thinking about us—no matter what the scale, mirror, tag size, or others say about us (Psalms 45:11; 139).
- He loves us even when we feel unloved or unlovable (Jeremiah 31:3).

When we fail and sin, we can confidently come to Him, knowing that He invites us, welcomes us, accepts us, and forgives us. We can also trust that as we fall on Him, He will change us. While the enemy convicts us of our sins to drive us to shame and guilt, God convicts us of sin in order to change us and make us whole and holy.

When we worry that we're not doing enough—not providing, accomplishing, or contributing enough—we can talk to Him. He promises that His yoke is easy (see Matthew 11:28–30). He will remind us that our value does not come from what we do but comes from whose we are. God is enough, even when we're not.

Others may not invite us, include us, or show any interest in us. He invites us to come boldly. He's available twenty-four hours a day, seven days a week, to listen. He hears beyond our words to our hearts. Even when we can't put words to what we're thinking or feeling, He gets us.

We need to take these truths to heart. We need to believe what God says about us instead of what the enemy says. We need to live it—not just say we believe it in our heads—and act like it. We need to talk like we believe it. We need to keep reminding ourselves. We need to post the truths that speak into the areas we battle the most on our mirrors and computer screens. We need to make the Scriptures that speak to our wounds as our home screens on our devices. We need to use key words from the Bible's promises that remind us of who we are as our passwords for our accounts as persistent reminders.

Accepting His grace and believing His love bring freedom from shame. Coming to Him and believing He is enough when we're not enable us to live encouraged lives instead of discouraged ones. Surrendering our strife allows us to finally rest in Him and find peace. His enoughness brings courage and hope when we feel hopeless. It empowers us to be the people He designed us to be instead of shadows of ourselves.

I'm not saying it's easy. It's a battle. And as you start the journey of finding you're enough in God instead of in your accomplishments, education, stuff, size, mirror, or relationships, the enemy will attack. He will be relentless in his attempts to keep you focused on yourself and the ways you just don't measure up or do enough. But my friend, you can never make yourself be enough—no matter how hard you try. There will always be something else to achieve or someplace where you don't get it right or quite measure up. There will always be someone who can do it better or someone whose critical words will crush your heart.

It's time we start telling ourselves the truth. We cannot make ourselves enough. But *He* is enough. His love makes us enough. He accepts us. He gives us value and purpose. He is enough!

Your story
- How have you allowed God to be enough in your life? How have you tried to be enough on your own?
- What are the areas in which you've battled the most? What would it change if you gave these areas to God and allowed Him to be enough?
- How can you start to remind yourself to let your not enoughness drive you to God instead of letting it drive you?
- What is one promise you want to begin reminding yourself of over and over until you really get it?

God is enough
God is enough even when you're not.

Promise
"And He said to me, 'My grace is sufficient for you, for My strength is made perfect in weakness.' Therefore most gladly I will rather boast in my infirmities, that the power of Christ may rest upon me" (2 Corinthians 12:9).

Prayer
O Father God, You are enough. I know this is true, but I don't always live like it or believe it at the core of who I am. Lord, forgive me for trying to be enough by myself. I'm tired of trying. I want to find my value and enoughness in You alone— not in the accomplishments that push me to do more or in the scale or mirror that all too often determines whether I'm going to have a good day or bad day. Help me to fall on You. Let my feelings of not being enough or doing enough drive me to You and not just drive me to try harder or do more on my own. God, help me to remember that You are enough, even when I'm not. In Jesus' name, amen.

---

1. Stasi Eldredge, *Free to Be Me* (Colorado Springs, CO: David C. Cook, 2014), 40.

Chapter 8

The God

Most of us know the Creation story.

In the beginning God created the heavens and the earth. The earth was without form, and void; and darkness was on the face of the deep. And the Spirit of God was hovering over the face of the waters.

Then God said, "Let there be light"; and there was light. And God saw the light, that it was good; and God divided the light from the darkness. God called the light Day, and the darkness He called Night. So the evening and the morning were the first day (Genesis 1:1–5).

God spoke, and our world was created. Have you ever thought about what that looked like? Do you picture a deep, booming voice cutting through the darkness, commanding light, and suddenly, there is light? The next day God's deep, booming voice decrees the heavens to appear and then land and seas on the following day. Then He starts filling these places with beauty and creatures. Do you imagine one word from God, and immediately, thousands of different types of trees, flowers, grasses, and shrubs appear all at once? All with just a word! Creation reveals an amazing God!

I believe God spoke and our world was created and filled with unbelievable beauty. But I like to imagine it a little differently than simply a loud, commanding voice. I picture God—the Father, the Son, and the Holy Spirit—having a conversation, getting excited, and being creative. I imagine joy and fun were part of creating the world. Just imagine a little with me.

The Father speaks a horse into existence. "Let's create a horse with sturdy legs that can gallop powerfully across a field and let it have a beautiful palomino color, with a lighter mane and tail. Let the tail be long enough to flow in the wind as it runs. Let's give it a gentle nicker that will steal the hearts of teenage girls." (I know Adam and Eve weren't created yet, but God said we were planned before He even began creation; see Ephesians 1:4.)

"Wait. Let's create some that have black-and-white or brown-and-white spots, and make them a little smaller—ponies," suggests the Son.

The Holy Spirit speaks, "Hey, I have an idea! Let's create one with black-and-white stripes that even go into its mane!"

The Son is getting excited. "I love it! Let's give ponies a bit more personality than horses and make them a bit stockier and ornerier."

"What if We create a miniature version of a horse," the Father laughs. "Women are going to love tiny things."

As They speak, the world is filled with horses, ponies, and zebras. A variety of colors and sizes of horses gallop across the new, freshly created fields filled with an assortment of grasses, grains, and wildflowers. And zebras roam next to lions and elephants.

God goes on to create lions, tigers, bears, groundhogs, hedgehogs, and porcupines. And how did the platypus happen?

When They are done and the world is alive with animals, the Three look at Their work and smile. "It is good."

Does the thought of God getting excited, having fun together, and enjoying speaking the world and all that is in it into creation bring a smile to your face? It does to mine. I love to imagine Creation happening with God—the Father, Son and Holy Spirit—being excited and filled with joy and laughter while working together, taking great pleasure in speaking Their creation into existence.

God created us with joy too!

I believe God took the same joy and care in creating each and every one of us. I believe They gathered together and excitedly talked about you as They decided who you would be, what you would be passionate about, and how you would impact the world.

"Let's give this child her mom's love of music," says the Father.

"Oh, and let's add her dad's sense of humor," shares the Holy Spirit.

The Father looks at Him. "Her dad has a sense of humor?" They laugh together over the quirkiness of the humor They gave your dad.

"What if We throw in a bit of her great-great-great-aunt Matilda's passion for gardens and flowers," the Son adds. "Her family will wonder where it came from." Again, They laugh together.

"Let's add a smear of freckles across her cheeks and nose to remind her of her granny," the Spirit suggests.

"She's going to need a lot of energy to keep up with all of those kids!"

On and on the conversation goes as They create you, taking great joy and delight in planning who you will be. Then They get a bit serious. "What part of Us will we give her?" One of Them asks. They always get to this moment in each person's story. We were all created in Their image. We each reflect God.

"Let's give her a heart for children," the Father decides. "They will need her compassionate ways."

"Yes," the Son agrees. "And she will bring fun into their lives with her creativity."

"And her dad's humor," laughs the Holy Spirit.

Please forgive me if you read this and think I'm making light of God or making

Him too human. That is not my intention at all. I believe there was a holy reverence in creation—in the beginning—and for each one of us. I am in awe of God and His amazing love that created with such detail and extravagance. I also believe God created with joy, love, and excitement. He planned this. He wanted this. He wanted us. He wanted you.

David found joy in this idea. He, too, believed that God was intentional in creating each one of us. He wrote,

> You made all the delicate, inner parts of my body
>   and knit me together in my mother's womb.
> Thank you for making me so wonderfully complex!
>   Your workmanship is marvelous—how well I know it.
> You watched me as I was being formed in utter seclusion,
>   as I was woven together in the dark of the womb.
> You saw me before I was born.
>   Every day of my life was recorded in your book.
> Every moment was laid out
>   before a single day had passed.
> How precious are your thoughts about me, O God.
>   They cannot be numbered!
> I can't even count them;
>   they outnumber the grains of sand!
> And when I wake up,
>   you are still with me
> (Psalm 139:13–18, NLT).

God saw you before you were born.
He knit you together, created you, and planned you.
He wrote your story in His Book.
He thinks about you—yes, you—more than you can even comprehend.
Isn't that amazing?

The God of the universe, the Creator of heaven and earth, the Ruler and King who always was and always is, the Mighty Warrior—this huge, bigger-than-we-can-comprehend God—created us with intentionality and delight.

Why?

Because He wanted us. He wanted you. He loves you; He really, truly, deeply loves you.

He knew this world would impact us. He knew we would too often choose other things and people over Him. He knew that we would demand our own way instead of seeking His and we would want things to turn out a certain way in our lives, but many times, that wouldn't happen. He understands our disappointments, our frustrations, and the ache in our heart for something more.

He also knew that others' sins would wound us. His heart aches for us and the wounds that go deep, changing our view of the world, ourselves, and His love. He hates the shame that causes us to hide and the ways we allow it to limit us and keep us from living abundant lives.

He knew the enemy would lie to us about who we are and who He is. He knew we would struggle and battle. Sin would become a wall between us. So, out of His great love for us, He had a plan. He sent His Son to take our place in death and pay our penalty in order to redeem us and enable us to live with Him for eternity. He sends His Spirit to work in our lives to bring healing, hope, and courage. He sends His angels to protect us. All of heaven is on our side and is fighting for us. I hope that on the other side of eternity we get to see the behind-the-scenes videos of our lives. I believe we will be overwhelmed when we finally understand all that God has done and is doing in our lives every single day.

God loves us more than anyone ever has or ever will, and because of this great love, God convicts us of sin. He speaks into our lives to rebuke our selfishness and the habits and actions that take us out of His will. He is our Father, and like a good parent, He disciplines us—not to punish us but to teach us and guide us to the life that is best for us. He knows the damage that sin and our self-focus do to our hearts, others, and our influence on the world around us. While God is love, His love draws us close, brings out the best in us, and convicts us when we're doing things that will hurt others or ourselves. But He convicts and disciplines with love in order to redeem and change us, never to shame or guilt us. When you're feeling shame and guilt, that's the enemy attempting to turn conviction into discouragement so that you beat yourself up and surrender. God's conviction and discipline will bring sadness or disappointment in ourselves, but it won't bring shame. God's goal is to draw us deeper and help us live the lives He originally planned for us. He longs to redeem and restore us and one day have us with Him for eternity where sin will no longer wound us or keep us from Him.

Even now, He is preparing our future home (John 14:1–3). I'm sure He's taking even more joy in preparing a place for us where sin will no longer impact us, and we will be with Him forever—and we will be able to see Him and hear Him.

My friend, He longs for us to believe His words of love and live like it. If we could believe that God loves us, He intentionally planned us, and He wants and delights in us—believe all of this at the core of who we are and let it become our identity—it would change our lives. How can you beat yourself up or think you're not enough if you truly believe God sees, knows, redeems, and loves you? How can you care and compete with others when you know that you are enough in Him? If we could grasp His love and the promise that He has a plan for our lives, created us with gifts to be used for His kingdom, we wouldn't struggle, thinking we have nothing to offer or that we can't make a difference.

God longs for us to believe we are who He says we are and that He is who His Word reveals He is. He wants us to recognize the lie that it's up to us to make ourselves be enough and live the truth that He is enough. He wants our not enoughness to drive us to Him.

Lord *and* Savior

Our not enoughness brings us to God in the first place. As we recognize that we are sinners, we understand our need for Jesus, believe that He died for us, commit our lives to Him, and accept Him as Savior. Many of us publicly proclaim this love for God and commitment to Him by being baptized in front of our family and friends. We are amazed that He accepts us and welcomes us.

But all too often, we walk out of the baptismal tank and into a life where we struggle to make ourselves enough. We attempt to do it ourselves, trying hard to get it right, only to fail. We beat ourselves up for messing up and then try harder.

I remember learning about God as a little girl. I attended a Good News Club in my neighbor's yard. Each summer morning for a week, a group of teens gathered us children under a shady tree and told us stories. One was an exciting mission story that ended just as things were getting good. We'd be on the edge of our seats, wondering what was going to happen next, only to have to come back the next day to find out. And there were always stories about God. I really don't remember the details of their stories. I'm sure we probably sang a few songs too. I can't even tell you the names of the young people who met with us each day. But I'll never forget learning that God loved *me*.

I was this super shy, scrawny girl. I was the oldest of five kids, with four younger brothers born before I turned five (the first one arrived before my first birthday, and the second one came before my second), and Mom had her hands full. Dad worked long hours to provide for us—sometimes working a second job in the evenings. I didn't think anyone ever noticed me.

Yet these kids said that God loved me and that I didn't have to do anything to make Him notice me or love me. He just did. I didn't have to practice my clarinet, which my mom and music teacher thought I should do every day, even though I would rather play outside. I didn't have to get straight As in math. (Not my favorite subject!) God just loved me.

I remember listening as the teens invited kids to come forward and accept Jesus as their Savior. I wanted to but was too shy to go forward. So I listened from under the tree as they prayed, then I ran home and up the stairs to my bedroom where I got down on my knees and prayed, inviting Jesus to be my Savior.

It'd be a few years before our family moved and a local church offered to pick up my brothers and me and take us to church. I quickly got involved in the youth group, even becoming a peer leader. I loved God and enjoyed our youth group. I knew that I wanted to walk with God and serve Him for the rest of my life. I even hoped to marry a pastor so I could be involved in ministry. (I didn't realize that there were lots of ways to do ministry or there were ways for women to be involved outside of teaching the children's classes.)

But there was a problem.

While I loved God and wanted to serve Him, I didn't like myself very much. I tried hard to be good and do things "right." When I succeeded, I thanked God for what He was doing in my life. When I failed, I beat myself up for not being enough. I really tried—hard. I wanted to be a good person and a good Christian and tried doing everything I thought I needed to do. Eventually, discouragement, frustration, and weariness became my constant companions. I was exhausted by trying to look good on the outside while feeling hopeless on the inside.

One night in my college dorm room, I gave up. I remember praying and telling God how weary I was as I swallowed pills, then lay down and hoped death would bring rest. God was so incredibly gracious. He moved people and circumstances so that I was taken to the hospital the next evening—a full day after swallowing the handfuls of pills. It wasn't until the following afternoon that my heart stopped, but a team of doctors and nurses was right there to get it going again. One of those nurses stayed by my bedside until I woke up. She understood. She had come to that place once in her life too. Her story and presence were an encouragement to my weary heart. Yet it would take a few more months and a visit to my pastor before I would find real peace and understand the problem.

You see, while I had invited God to be my Savior, I hadn't asked Him to be Lord.

I was still in control of my life. I was trying to make myself be enough; I was trying to do good things on my own. I had a plan for my life, and while I asked God to bless it and guide me, I didn't really stop and ask Him what He wanted. I was trying to do things on my own, and it wasn't going so well.

I remember going for a walk after the visit with the pastor. Scripture and thoughts he had shared tumbled around in my head. Not far into the woods, I sunk down by a fallen tree and cried out to God. I gave Him everything. I told Him about the pain and battle in my heart. I shared my weariness of trying to do it all right and make myself good enough for Him and for others. I cried and asked Him to be not only my Savior but also the Lord of my life. I just couldn't do it on my own.

Peace filled my heart as I walked out of the woods and back into my life. My circumstances hadn't changed, but something in me had. I finally allowed my not enoughness to drive me to God instead of driving me to try harder to do more and be more. I made Him Lord of my life, surrendering control and my ideas of what life should look like. I began to recapture that little-girl belief that He loves me and allowed that to be enough. I was ready to trust that He was working in me and through me, and He would continue convicting, changing, growing, and guiding me. There are days when I struggle and battle with the feeling that I am not enough. I wrestle with the way life looks, wishing for things to go the way I think would be best. But He is always right there, gently calling me to let go and surrender to Him.

How about you? Are you ready to let your not enoughness drive you to a God who is enough?

Your story

- As you imagine God intentionally planning and creating you, how does it change the way you see yourself and your purpose and life?
- Have you invited Jesus to be your Savior? If not, are you ready? Stop right now, and talk to Him. Thank Him for His love and sacrifice. Tell Him you recognize your need for a Savior, and surrender your life to Him. Contact your local pastor, and talk to God about your decision and baptism—making your new commitment public for family and friends to witness.
- Have you surrendered your will and your desires for your life to God and asked Him to be Lord? If not, are you ready to spend time with God, surrendering your will, your pain, your hopes, your disappointments, your dreams, your failures, and your successes, and ask Him to be Lord of your life instead of yourself?

God is enough

God is enough to be both Savior and Lord of your life.

Promise

"I have been crucified with Christ; it is no longer I who live, but Christ lives in me; and the life which I now live in the flesh I live by faith in the Son of God, who loved me and gave Himself for me" (Galatians 2:20).

Prayer

Father God, thank You for all You have done for me. You thought about me, planned me, designed me, and created me to reflect You. You sent Your Son to die for me so that I could be with You for eternity. I know it and believe it, yet it's hard to totally understand. Thank You for being my Savior and Redeemer. Father, please be Lord of my life too! Forgive me for trying to do this on my own. Thank You that You invite me to surrender and find rest. Yes! I want that rest in You. I give You my disappointments, my failures, my sin, and the sins I don't want to surrender; please give me the desire and willingness to surrender everything. Father, take away the fear the enemy wants me to feel. Help me to remember that You have a good plan, not to harm me but to bring me hope. I trust You; help me to trust You more. God, I surrender my dreams and my vision for the way I think life should be. Plant Your dreams in my heart, and fill me with purpose and passion in You. Lord, not my will, but Yours please! Thank You that my not enoughness can drive me to You and remind me of my need for You. Every time the enemy tempts me to focus on not being enough, let it be a reminder to surrender to You! Thank You for loving me with an everlasting love and for pursuing me with kindness. In Jesus' name, amen.

Chapter 9

The Pursuit

But He needed to go through Samaria" (John 4:4). He needed to go—not "wanted to go" nor "should go." Jesus *needed* to go through Samaria.

It doesn't seem like a big deal as we read it, but the Jews who heard this story wouldn't understand. The Samaritans were despised. Most Jews would travel three days out of their way to avoid going through Samaria. They believed it would make them unclean. And if they did go through Samaria, they would abstain from interacting with the people living there. There was a history of hate for the Samaritans. Most Jews believed that Samaritans weren't good enough—they didn't get life and faith right enough.

Yet Jesus *needed* to go through Samaria. Why?

As we read the story, we discover it's because one of Jesus' girls is fighting a battle. She believes she is not enough and is too much, she hides, and she tries to fill those deep needs of her heart herself. He needs her to know that He is enough.

Jesus' love is the driving force behind the need to break the rules, ignore what others think, and get to a daughter who needs Him. She needs to know who she is in Him and needs to know who God really is. His love compels Him. He knows she's out there and He must go to her. His heart and love will not allow Him to do anything else. Jesus is always willing to go out of His way for us.

Middle of an ordinary day
"So He came to a city of Samaria which is called Sychar, near the plot of ground that Jacob gave to his son Joseph. Now Jacob's well was there. Jesus therefore, being wearied from His journey, sat thus by the well. It was about the sixth hour" (verses 5, 6). Sychar is located almost midway between Judea and Galilee, close to the mountains. So Jesus and His disciples have traveled to the very heart of Samaria. They arrive at Jacob's well, which is a known landmark. It's a resting place for travelers and a place to refresh. It's also a social gathering location for the community. Each morning women come for the water they need for the day ahead. But they also come for more than water. We all know what happens when women get together, right? They talk. It is a time of connecting, catching up, sharing gossip, and friendships before they tackle their to-do lists for the day.

Jesus arrives at the sixth hour. (People didn't have clocks or watches then, so time was counted by the sun.) The sixth hour is six hours after sunrise—about noon. It is a hot time of day with the sun overhead, so the well is a quiet place. Everyone has come for their water and gone. No one ventures out at noon. It is hot, and people are busy with their tasks. Jesus sits by the well while His disciples go into town for food. He sits and waits for her.

She comes to the well, expecting no one to be there. She is avoiding other women because she is hurting and feels like she is not enough. She used to come in the morning. But as her life turned out differently than she expected or ever wanted, the women, maybe once friends, began to whisper, avoid her, and gossip about her. She could feel their stares, knew they were talking about her, and felt their disapproval.

Friends, when we women do relationships right—when we encourage, care for, and speak words of hope and courage to one another—we can be sources of strength for each other. But we don't always do friendships right. We become like those mean middle-school girls so often depicted on TV and in movies: girls who gossip and avoid and exclude others. You know the type. Many of you reading this have been hurt by other women, their words, and their judgment. You learn to avoid them and pretend like their rejection doesn't matter and that you don't really need them. You keep busy so that you don't have time for friendships and keep people at a distance to avoid getting hurt. Yet deep inside, we were all created with a need to be loved, accepted, and seen.

This woman's heart was as empty as the water pot she carried.

When does she realize Jesus is there? The lone Man sitting by the well. Does she consider turning around and avoiding this encounter?

As she approaches, she can tell by His clothes that He is a Jew. Is she curious as to why a Jew is in Samaria? She knows that a Jew won't speak to a Samaritan man, let alone speak to a woman—and she is a Samaritan woman! He'll ignore her, and she'll be able to get in, get her water, and get out.

And then He speaks to her.

I love this story! Don't miss this truth—Jesus knew she was battling with feeling like she wasn't enough, wasn't wanted, didn't fit in, and didn't belong. Jesus knew that she was battling shame and guilt and a broken heart. He *needs* to get to her. So He shows up in the middle of her ordinary day. She shows up in the middle of her hurt and loneliness. The women avoid her and gossip. The men use her. But Jesus waits to speak hope, value, love, and purpose into her life. And He does the same thing for us! Watch for Him. Look for Him. He shows up in the middle of our everyday lives, speaking courage and love.

Just yesterday, discouragement hung like a cloud over me as I started my day curled up in a chair to hang out with God. After reading Scripture and praying, I checked my email before heading into work and found a friend had sent a devotional that spoke to her that morning. The message brought tears to my eyes. Getting in the car, I turned on some music and caught the words to a song playing from the CD just as I was switching to the radio—and the exact same song was playing, reminding me that God says we are loved even when we don't feel loved. He was making sure I heard the message regardless of whether I turned on the CD or the radio. Wow. At the bottom of my hill, I stopped and saw an amazing sunrise with colors and clouds and rays of sunlight streaming powerfully from behind the fading darkness. It was a visual representation of what He was doing in my heart. My friends, God waits for us in our everyday lives—not just at church or during Bible studies—right in the middle of work, chores, and errands. His love compels Him to persistently and relentlessly pursue us.

The invitation

"Jesus said to her, 'Give Me a drink' " (verse 7). I know that might sound like a command, as though Jesus is treating her like a servant without even saying hello first. But that's our culture hearing it. In her culture, asking someone for a drink of water was an invitation to engage. Sharing a drink or meal showed respect and acceptance. It was a request you didn't refuse. This wasn't about Jesus wanting something from her. It was about what He wants to give her. He meets her in this moment and invites her into a relationship. He is offering her what her heart is longing for—acceptance, belonging, love, value, and purpose.

Not enough

"How is it that You, being a Jew, ask a drink from me, a Samaritan woman?" (verse 9). Do you hear the hurt and sarcasm? The words laced with bitterness and shame? She doesn't give Him the asked-for drink. She doesn't believe she's good enough to meet His request. She tries to point out the obvious to Him. He's a Jew. She's a Samaritan *and* a woman. Two strikes. In her heart, she knows the third strike and is probably thinking, *And if You only knew me, knew who I really am and the life I'm living, if You knew me, You would never ask me for a drink.* Strike three, and you're out!

Jesus knows the woman's heart, knows her shame, and knows that she is battling. Jesus knows she is longing to be loved and hopes for a purpose, but she believes she isn't enough and thinks she'll never get it right or be good enough for anyone. He continues to persist.

"If you knew the gift of God, and who it is who says to you, 'Give Me a drink,' you would have asked Him, and He would have given you living water" (verse 10). *"If you knew."* While she's thinking if He really knew her, He wouldn't want anything to do with her, He knows that if she knew who He really was, she'd want what He offers. He knows her, but she doesn't know Him—not yet. How could she? She never expected God to show up in the middle of the day and talk to her and offer to satisfy her heart's desires. Jesus is offering her more than she understands. He and His love are bigger than she can comprehend.

Isn't this true of us? How often do we really expect God to show up in the middle of our ordinary days? In the middle of our ordinariness? My friend Diane shared how God sent her a song just when she needed it—the perfect words and message right in the middle of a battle with the very issue with which she was dealing. It surprised her that God would orchestrate the radio broadcast just for her in that moment. It surprises us because often that's not our human experience. We're more likely to feel unseen, forgotten, rejected, and like no one understands or cares. Yet there He is for her, for Diane, for me, and for you.

Notice the promise in Jesus' words? "You would have asked Him, and He *would* have given you living water." *Would.* Not "maybe" or "God will consider the request." God *would* give if she asked.

"Would have given *you* living water." He would give *her*—not just everyone else but her. How many times have I heard women say that they know God will do things for other people, but they aren't sure He will do these things for them? Or how often have people asked me to pray for them because God listens to me more than them? If you only knew who He is! He will answer your prayers. Every Bible promise is yours. Every spiritual blessing in heaven is yours (Ephesians 1:3). God loves *you*. The enemy will attempt to do all he can to cause us to believe that God loves us if we do this or that, if we measure up, if we get it right, or if we are enough. Not true, my friend. God just loves you—right now, completely, more than you can imagine or understand. He knows you're not enough. He still chose you. And if you trust Him, He will work in your life to change you, grow you, and give you purpose and fill those longings to be loved, accepted, and belong.

His message is clear. You may think you're not enough, but God is enough.

Too much

The woman's wounds run deep. Jesus' words invite but don't completely break down the walls she's built.

"Sir, You have nothing to draw with, and the well is deep" (verse 11).

Can I translate that for you? Sir, I'm too much, too needy. You don't have what it takes to help me.

We might never say it quite like that, but deep down, it's sometimes what we believe: *I'll never get it right; I'll never be enough.* We say we believe God can move mountains and calm storms, but all too often, we fear that He can't change us, can't make us enough, and can't meet the deep needs of our hearts. We will always feel lonely, rejected, or filled with shame.

But Jesus doesn't give up on her. I love how He relentlessly pursues her heart.

"Whoever drinks of this water will thirst again, but whoever drinks of the water that I shall give him will never thirst" (verse 13). Translation: you can keep trying to satisfy your heart with things or people or your own efforts; however, they will never meet your needs. But I can. Your need is not too much. You are not too much. I have what it takes to completely satisfy your heart and make you whole and holy and Mine.

What Jesus offers will satisfy the woman's soul and fill her heart. "The peace of God, which surpasses all understanding," and the "fullness of joy" will give her abundant life (Philippians 4:7; Psalm 16:11). She's been trying to fill those longings on her own. Her method has been men, one right after another. But the one-right-after-another part adds to her belief that she's not enough and that her need is too great. This leaves her feeling shame and rejection. She has become the talk of the town—avoided by women and watched by men—and not for good reasons. She feels more alone and unwanted than ever.

Can you relate? Have you tried to find things to meet the needs of your heart? Maybe it hasn't been men—though many girls believe that having a man love them will make things better, so they give guys whatever they want in hopes of being loved. Perhaps you try to fill those longings with chocolate or by eating away the emotions with any type of food. Maybe it's people pleasing, looking good, or having the right clothes or house. Maybe it's striving to accomplish and make an impact and a difference, thinking if you can just do more and be more, then life will be different. Maybe you watch your social-media notifications for verification that you're enough; you let Facebook and Twitter likes determine how you feel about yourself today. Or you base what you think about yourself on the scale, the size written on a tag, or the mirror. It's exhausting and discouraging living like that, isn't it?

The woman is tired of trying so hard and never getting what she needs. Her heart wants what Jesus is offering and wants to believe that it's true: He can satisfy and heal the broken places of her heart and make her enough.

"Sir, give me this water, that I may not thirst, nor come here to draw" (verse 15). Yes, please! I want what You're offering! I don't want to be thirsty anymore. I don't want the loneliness and rejection of coming alone in the middle of the day to get water, avoiding the stares and whispers and reminders that I am not enough. I don't want to walk past the men at the gate as I come and as I return, seeing them smile and wonder whether they can have me next. I don't want the daily reminders that I am not enough or that I'm too much. I just want peace. I want love. I want hope.

Her look is desperate yet hopeful. Could this Stranger help?

No more hiding

Jesus' next words had to cut the woman like a knife, take her breath away, and dash her hopes.

"Go, call your husband, and come here" (verse 16). *Husband*—the very thing she was using in an attempt to fill that empty place in her heart and that longing to be loved. Jesus knew the thirstiest part of her soul. We don't know her complete story. We do know she had five husbands and was now living with a man who hadn't married her. We don't know what happened to the first five husbands. Did they die? Divorce her? Why did men keep marrying her? Finally, no one would marry her, so she took what she could get and was with a man who wouldn't commit. Sometimes when we don't feel like we are enough and we're hungry to be loved, we will do anything to fill that need:

- accept less than we want or is good for us,
- do whatever we can to make people like us, or
- try to be who we think others want us to be instead of being ourselves.

We attempt to look the part, go along, settle for less—settle for anything.

Imagine the terror in the woman's heart. She's so close to getting what she longs for, but what if He learns the truth and walks away? What if He finds out who she really is and what she's done, and then He won't give her this living water? In an instant, she decides to hide or fake the truth about who she is. Many of us do it. We try to cover up our failures, our sins, and our disappointments. We smile and act like there's nothing wrong and everything is good. We put on our church clothes and church smiles and greet each other like everything is great:

"How are you doing?"

"I'm fine; how are you?"

"Fine."

We hide the battles, the struggles, the discouragement, and the fears. We lie about who we are and how we're doing because we don't want to be judged; we believe no one cares; or we fear that if people discovered who we really are, they wouldn't like us. And shame covers us a little more every time we hide.

"I have no husband" (verse 17).

I love how Jesus responds. Imagine a small smile playing on His face and the gentle way He speaks to her: "You have well said, 'I have no husband,' for you have had five husbands, and the one whom you now have is not your husband; in that you spoke truly" (verse 18).

Whoa! He knows! He knows everything about her! And yet He doesn't walk away. He doesn't shame or scold or accuse or rebuke her.

"In that you spoke truly." Is Jesus being playful? You didn't really lie, did you? You told the truth, just not the whole truth.

Relationship, not rules

Jesus just keeps pursuing her, taking her past all the layers of not being enough, being too much, and hiding. He is digging deep to reach her heart, convicting her of sin, and calling her to something different. He is drawing her to Him—to a relationship.

But she does what many of us do when we're struggling. She doesn't want to go there. She doesn't want to deal with her pain and guilt and shame and sin. She's feeling exposed. So she attempts to cover up by going to the rules: tell me what to do, and I'll get it right and do it all.

Rules are often easier than dealing with our messy hearts. If we keep focusing on the rules, we don't have to deal with the sin and the relationship. We don't have to look at our hearts. We don't have to really look at ourselves, admit our weaknesses, and allow God to do the work of restoring us. Rules are easier and safer. They are something to focus on and try hard at. Get it right.

Really, if she could just get it right, she'd be accepted. Right? If she was just good enough, maybe she would be loved and included? She doesn't really know God, but she knows religion, so that's where she hides next.

"Sir, I perceive that You are a prophet" (verse 19). Samaritans believed that Moses was the only prophet, so her statement is huge. She recognizes that the Man before her is not an ordinary Jewish man. Jesus is moving her away from what she's always believed to the possibility that there is something more.

"Our fathers worshiped on this mountain, and you Jews say that in Jerusalem is the place where one ought to worship" (verse 20). So who's right? Where should we worship? Tell me, and I'll do it. But let's not talk about the husband thing.

Jesus could have argued with her about doctrine and rules. He could have gone down this path and made sure she believed the right ways and places to worship. But Jesus is going for the one thing needed—getting her to believe the right things about God, who He is, who she is in Him, and what He's called her to. Jesus wants her heart. He wants a relationship with her. He wants her to find that God is enough.

"Jesus said to her, 'Woman, believe Me, the hour is coming when you will neither on this mountain, nor in Jerusalem, worship the Father' " (verse 21). Hear the tenderness in His voice, the love, as He draws her, speaking words that possibly no one else has ever used—or at least not in a long time—as He pursues her.

Jesus could have used any name for God as He spoke. But He chose *Father*. It implies belonging, connection, and a relationship. He goes on to tell the woman that what God is really seeking are those who are really seeking Him. Religion is not about getting it right; it's about getting to Him. It's about worshiping—focusing on—God. It's about God being enough, not her failure to be enough or her trying to be enough.

Believe

She wants to believe. " 'I know that Messiah is coming' (who is called Christ). 'When He comes, He will tell us all things' " (verse 25). Can she believe Jesus? Is it really that simple? Worship God? Trust God? Seek God with all of her heart? All of her life she's been taught what she should do and shouldn't do. She knows she's not measuring up. Could it be true that God knows all about her and invites her anyway? That He is enough?

"I who speak to you am He," Jesus reveals Himself as the Messiah (verse 26). This is the only place and the only person in all four Gospels to whom He speaks it so clearly. I AM the I AM. I wonder how He tells her. Does He quietly whisper it to her like He is sharing a secret? Are His eyes full of joy and hope that she will believe as He proclaims His identity? He reveals Himself and invites her into a relationship. He invites her to believe that even after five husbands and living with a man who isn't her husband, even after hiding and avoiding, feeling shame and rejection, settling for less in order to get something, God loves her and is enough for her broken, needy heart. He hasn't revealed Himself to the Jews. He chooses a Samaritan woman with a bad reputation—an outcast among the outcast. Doesn't that give you hope?

"The woman then left her waterpot, went her way into the city, and said to the men, 'Come, see a Man who told me all things that I ever did. Could this be the Christ?' Then they went out of the city and came to Him" (verses 28–30). Her water pot is still empty, but her heart is not. It is filled with joy and hope. He knows all about her, yet He still accepts her! Now she's the one who needs to go—go to the very people whom she had been avoiding and tell them about the Man at the well. That's what happens when you discover that God is enough and that He loves you, pursues you, knows all about you, and accepts you. You are compelled to tell others. You want others to discover the joy and hope. You want others to know that God loves them too.

"And many of the Samaritans of that city believed in Him because of the word of the woman who testified, 'He told me all that I ever did' " (verse 39). She becomes the first evangelist.

Purpose—you discover it when you discover who you are in Christ.

Relentlessly, persistently pursued by love

The woman's story is ours, isn't it? The details are different, but the themes are the same.

Jesus' love compels Him to pursue us. He came and died for us, but He didn't stop there. He pursues us in the middle of our ordinary days, waits for us to come, and invites us to know the Father.

He knows all about us. He knows where we're not enough and the places we feel like we're too much or too needy. He knows the ways we try to fill the needs of our hearts ourselves and the ways we try to make ourselves enough, or at least make ourselves look like we're enough. And He invites us to discover Him, discover more of Him—more than enough.

He is pursuing you. This book is just one small way. Are you ready to discover a God who is enough for your thirsty heart?

Your story
- What parts of the Samaritan woman's story do you relate to the most?
- Have you avoided friendships or social engagements?
- What have you run to in an attempt to fill the needs of your heart?
- How have you felt too much?
- Do you remember ways that you've seen God pursuing you?
- What is He speaking into your heart through this story?

God is enough
God is enough to relentlessly and persistently pursue us even when we're hiding.

Promise

"But now, this is what the LORD says—
    he who created you, Jacob,
    he who formed you, Israel:
'Do not fear, for I have redeemed you;
    I have summoned you by name; you are mine.
When you pass through the waters,
    I will be with you;
and when you pass through the rivers,
    they will not sweep over you.
When you walk through the fire,
    you will not be burned;
    the flames will not set you ablaze.
For I am the LORD your God,
    the Holy One of Israel, your Savior' "
(Isaiah 43:1–3, NIV).

Prayer

Father, thank You for this powerful story of Your love and pursuit. Your love is amazing and more than we can comprehend. You know all about us, yet You come for us, not with rebuke or shame but with love and conviction. You redeem and restore. You call us to things bigger than ourselves. Thank You for so many stories in Your Word of people who were not enough on their own, yet You loved them and made them enough for the purpose for which You created them. You didn't wait for them to be enough; You invited them into a relationship with You that made them enough. Thank You for doing the same for us. It's amazing that You *want* a relationship with us—a relationship—not just what we can do for You. You want us to know You and enjoy You. And You want us to believe that You know and enjoy us. Guide us. Help us discover more of You as we continue this journey! In Jesus' name, amen.

Part 3

Discovering the Enoughness of God

A woman in her glory, a woman of beauty, is a woman who is not striving to become beautiful or worthy or enough. She knows in her quiet center where God dwells that he finds her beautiful, has deemed her worthy, and in him, she is enough.

—John and Stasi Eldredge, *Captivating*

It's time to learn the weapons and strategies for the battle and discover a God who fights for us.

Chapter 10

The One Thing Needed

"O ne thing is needed" (Luke 10:42).

I wonder what Martha thought when she heard Jesus' words: "But one thing is needed." She has been trying so hard to impress, working to show that she is enough despite the thoughts in her head saying she isn't. She is angry and jealous that Mary isn't helping but is sitting and listening while she is working hard—and comparing and competing. Martha's thoughts are swirling around as the enemy slowly tempts her to think that Jesus doesn't care. All of her hard work and no one, not even Jesus, notices. Doesn't Jesus care how hard she is working? Can she really trust Him to know what she needs?

Jesus understands. His heart aches for her to find rest and peace in Him. He longs for feelings of not being enough to drive her to His feet, like they have Mary. He calls her name twice to get her attention, making sure she is looking at Him and hears His words not only with her ears but also with her heart. He doesn't want her to miss His invitation.

"You are worried and troubled about many things" (verse 41). He sees her. He's letting her know He understands what's happening inside her heart. The Greek verb translated "worried" is *merimnaō*, and it means "to be anxious" and to "look out for."[1] It's the same word used in the challenge of Matthew 6:25: "Do not worry about your life, what you will eat or drink; or about your body, what you will wear" (NIV). The word *troubled* is translated from the Greek verb *thorybazō*; it was most commonly used in reference to being "troubled in mind, disquieted," and disturbed.[2]

Jesus recognizes that Martha's heart is in an angry uproar, fighting between longing to sit at His feet and striving to prove herself. She is anxious to do it right, get it right, and be enough for Him.

Jesus invites her to trust Him, trust His love for her, and trust that He is enough.

We know that she chooses to trust Him. She chooses to stop striving and start sitting. But I doubt that it was an instant switch. She had to wrestle it through. When you've spent much of your life feeling like you're not enough and trying hard to be enough, do enough, and look good enough, change doesn't happen instantaneously. Jesus tells her that Mary has chosen this good part that can't be taken away (see verse 42). This choice isn't a one-and-done deal. We have to keep choosing daily—sometimes hourly—this one thing that is needed.

What is that one thing? We talked about it in an earlier chapter. The one thing is time with Jesus: sitting at His feet, getting to know Him as intimately as a human being can know God, and choosing to make time with God more important than anything else in our lives.

It's hard. Many of us attend a church service or a retreat and are convicted that we need to spend time with God. Speakers talk about their quiet time and challenge us to get up early and spend time with God. They tell us the difference journaling has made in their lives. Others talk about the importance of reading the Bible from cover to cover in a year.

We go home determined to get up early and spend time with God. It's what we should do, right?

It might go well for a day or two, but the enemy doesn't want us to spend time with God. It will be a battle. We may not even recognize the enemy's opposition. We oversleep one morning. We need to get to work early for a meeting the next. One thing after another pops up to distract and discourage us. Or we manage to take the time and begin reading in Genesis, but it's all so familiar that we don't expect to find anything new, so we just skim through. We hit a book such as Numbers and just don't see the point. We encounter passages we don't understand and struggle to even want to keep reading. Before we know it, it's been a week since we've even attempted to spend time with God. And we beat ourselves up for our failure and for not being a good enough Christian.

Been there?

I have. I've also been at a place where I tried adding in everything anyone said I should do to spend time with God. I remember a time when I'd get up and have two different devotional books to read *and* also attempted to have time to read and study the Bible. Then there was prayer. I used a notebook someone gave me that divided up one's prayer list throughout the week. On Sunday, you would pray for family; on Monday, for friends; and on Tuesday, for . . . You get the idea. Then I'd pick up my journal and write out a prayer to God in letter form. I tried keeping this up day after day because these were all things that I thought I should be doing. Or at least, others had told me I should. My time with God had become a cumbersome checklist of things to do. I was exhausted and bored with it. Everything I was doing was good stuff, but it had become a checklist and not a relationship.

Choosing a relationship

Choosing to spend time with God was never intended to leave us exhausted or beating ourselves up for not doing enough or not getting it right. It wasn't meant to be a burden. Jesus invites, "Come to me, all you who are weary and burdened, and I will give you rest. Take my yoke upon you and learn from me, for I am gentle and humble in heart, and you will find rest for your souls. For my yoke is easy and my burden is light" (Matthew 11:28–30, NIV).

Time with God is about coming to know and trust Him more deeply every day. It's about finding rest from our striving and trying in Him. It's about a relationship. We *know* that it's about a relationship, but we want to do it right, so we make it about all the things we *should* do. We wonder whether we are doing enough. And it ends up being a burden.

We talked about this earlier, but it's important to remember that Jesus didn't tell Martha she *should* spend time with Him. He told her it was the one thing *needed*. *Needed* is a totally different word. When we don't do those things that we *should*, we feel guilty, but we aren't really motivated for long to keep trying to do them (or even start them). When we don't do those things that we *need* to, something falls apart or grows worse, and our lives are not the same.

When we don't spend time with God, the consequences are great; I don't mean to imply that God is angry with us for not hanging out with Him, but our hearts, minds, and lives are impacted. We lack peace in ourselves and our circumstances. We compare and compete with others. We doubt God's love. We don't trust Him to do what's best in our lives. Like Martha, we find ourselves worried and troubled about many things.

We need to choose to make time for a relationship with God *because we need it*. And then we need to make that time about growing a relationship with God, not a checklist of all the things we should be doing in order to get that relationship right. It's about reading the Bible in order to understand God and His plan for our lives and the way He speaks into our daily battles, discouragements, hopes, and dreams. It isn't about checking that we've read a certain amount of verses that day. It's about prayer that draws us closer to God and not just giving God a list of people and circumstances that we want Him to fix.

Our time with God is an opportunity to get to know the One who created us intentionally, loves us the most, and wants more for us than we can possibly want for ourselves.

Kayaks and rocking chairs

"When do you experience God the most?" I asked.

I was at a women's retreat, leading a seminar on spending time with God. I can still picture the room of women. One older woman sitting on the front row raised her hand. And I instantly stereotyped her and thought I knew what her answer would be. I figured she would say that she encountered God the most while sitting in her rocking chair, Bible in her lap, praying for her kids and grandkids. (My apologies to all older women reading this!) That was far from her answer.

"When I'm in my kayak out on the lake."

You go, girl! I, too, have experienced God from the quiet paddling of my kayak as I breathed in the beauty around me. Eagles flew overhead. A heron, scared up from its resting spot, croaked an unearthly complaint. The fall-colored trees were a blaze of reds and yellows. The quiet waves rocked against my small boat. I even experienced God in the rhythm of rowing.

I've experienced God's presence while hiking mountains and while breathing in the scent of Fraser firs. I've felt He was near when rounding a bend and encountering a bear on a trail in the Smokies, when coming upon a mama and baby moose grazing by a trail in the Rockies, and when standing at the top of Precipice Trail in Acadia National Park and looking out over the ocean. Such peace.

God has spoken powerfully to my heart at Pennsylvania's Longwood Gardens. Just driving through the gate brings me a sense of peace and expectation.

Music also has stopped me in my tracks and brought me to prayer and worship more than once. There have been moments when a song has driven me to my knees or spoken healing into my hurting heart. I remember jumping into my car one day while crying, feeling hurt and angry. The radio was already on when the car started up. The words of the song playing caught me off guard; they were exactly what I needed in that hard moment. New tears started, but this time they were ones of joy and prayer.

And there are mornings as I sit with my Bible and journal in hand by our front window, watching the sky become light, when God has spoken through His Word or in response to the prayers I've journaled.

I love that God speaks to us in so many different ways. He longs for a relationship with us. He wants it more than we do. And He invites us to choose this one most important thing.

Martha accepted His invitation. We don't know what that looked like for her. But we do know the impact it had on her. She may have wrestled with His words a bit. Wouldn't you? " 'One thing is needed?' Really? Just sitting and listening to You? That's all God expects? Can't I do more? Don't You want me to serve? Who is going to feed these guys if I don't?"

Note that Martha's service wasn't a problem. In John 12, we find her serving a meal. Service and hospitality were probably her gifts, and they are needed gifts. The problem was her heart. She thought her service would make her be enough. She was using her gifts to try to make herself of value in Jesus' eyes. He wanted her to know that she was loved and valuable just for being herself: God already called her His daughter and accepted her, and He alone makes her enough.

What can I do today?

Friends, we need to choose time with God and make it a priority in our lives. Forget all the things we think we should do in order to know Him, and recognize our need for Him. In Him, we will find peace, joy, and hope and will understand that we are enough. We need to skip the checklist and ask ourselves, *What can I do today to know God better?*

Make time for Him—not just early in the morning—throughout the day. Don't read Scripture simply to check Bible reading off a list, but read with the belief that God wants to speak to us, then stop and focus on what speaks to our hearts, looking to understand and apply it to our lives. Understand that our time with Him may not look the same every day. And that's OK. There may be days when we hunger for more of His Word and days when we are struggling and just need to sit quietly and let the music speak to our hearts. There may be moments when we need to get the kayak out or lace up our hiking boots.

Make time for a relationship with God, like we would with any friend. If we treated our friends like we treat God all too often, would they really be our friends? Think about it. If we said to a friend, "I'm going to get up early each morning and do this, this, and this and then hit the road and get busy," how would he or she respond? If we listened to a friend talk for five minutes, then we got up and said, "OK, time's up. I've done what I needed to do, and now it's time to get to work," would he or she feel heard? Would we be building a relationship? What if we did all the talking and just told our friends everything we needed from them or wanted them to do, but we never stopped to thank them for what they had done or listened to them; would they want to be our friends for long?

Fortunately for us, God is much more patient with us than we deserve. He doesn't give up or walk away. He just keeps nudging us to something more, longing to draw us closer, and giving us the desire for more of Him.

When I got to the point where my quiet time was something that I dreaded because of all the *shoulds*, I knew things had to change. I wanted more. I wanted to know God as deeply as I could. I wanted Him to speak into my life. I wanted Him to change me. So I chose a relationship and made a commitment to it. Spending time with God would be the highest priority of my day, but this time would be about knowing Him and not about checking a bunch of things off my to-do list.

I'm a morning person, so early morning devotions work best for me. But not everyone is a morning person, so early mornings may not be your best time of day to spend with God. My friend Jeanne is not a morning person. She's a woman who deeply loves God, and it shows in her life. She's one of the sweetest, most caring people I know. She has such a heart for others—but not a heart for the early morning! She chooses to spend her time with God in the evening. One day she laughingly told me that she had been reading her Bible and realized that early morning wasn't the best time to hang out with God. "The evening and the morning were the first day," she said. "So when I'm spending time with God in the evening, I *am* starting my day with Him." She has a point there.

The takeaway is to choose a time when you are at your best to listen to God. Jeanne thinks more clearly in the evening. I am more alert early in the morning. Both of us make our time with God a priority. Just commit to hanging out with God, and guard that time like you would any other appointment.

Close the door

Once you've committed to choosing the one thing that is needed, make that time about knowing God and building a relationship with Him. Make it about *your* relationship with Him. Do what connects you to God and draws you deeper. There are so many ways to spend this time with God:

- reading Scripture
- listening to an audio Bible
- singing or listening to music
- walking in nature
- art or Bible journaling
- praying
- reading what others have written

The point is to connect with God and let Him and His Word speak into your life, convicting, affirming, encouraging, and guiding you.

Guard this time. You'll have to battle for it. The enemy will try to distract you and keep you from it or cause you to make the time a burden you don't enjoy so that you avoid it. Don't let him win. Watch for his attacks.

I love my early morning time with God. There's something about the quiet just before the sun comes up and the house is asleep. I enjoy getting up, making myself a cup of tea, and curling up in the big chair by our front window. But as much as I love that time, I have to fight for it.

At one point, the battle was the gym. Going to the gym while on my way to work became an important part of my morning too. Exercise is important, right? My day began with time with God, then the gym, and off to the office. But there started to be more and more mornings when I only had time for one or the other. In those moments, I chose to try to do both, squeezing in time with God and the gym at the same time. I donned my workout clothes and prayed on the way to the gym. I listened to Christian podcasts while I worked out. Next, I listened to Christian radio and/or prayed on the way from the gym to the office. Then God convicted me that He wasn't getting my undivided attention. My workouts were the priority, and He was being squeezed in around them. Convicted, I decided that if I only had time for one or the other, the gym lost and God won. I wanted focused time with God. And when I got to the gym, I could still listen to podcasts and pray on my drive to work.

The enemy is relentless in his desire to distract us. He will keep trying. Even when we win one battle, the enemy will just try another angle.

I admit that my mind was not on the sermon one Sabbath morning. Our pastor was preaching a familiar passage, so my eyes wandered to the surrounding texts. One stopped me: "When you pray, go into your room, close the door and pray to your Father" (Matthew 6:6, NIV).

At that moment, God convicted my heart: "Close the door." I was suddenly aware that a lot of things were distracting me early in the morning. First, I'd put on the kettle for tea and then check Facebook and Instagram. But I was scrolling long after my tea had finished steeping. Or I'd get up and put a load of laundry in the washing machine, pick things up a bit around the house, and then prep for dinner so it would be quicker to cook when I got home in the evening. Before I knew it, it was time to leave for work, and I hadn't spent time with God or had a shortened time with Him because of all the distractions.

A lot of things were vying for my attention early in the morning. It was time to close the door and focus on God. I committed to closing the door—literally. I decided to have my time with God in my home office where I could go in and physically close the door. That simple act of closing the door reminded me to close the door on all the other things attempting to distract me. The closed door created a smaller, quieter space to hang out with God. I filled the area with things that reminded me of Him:

- A tiara that a friend sent me from Scotland. (My friend knew I teach little girls that they are God's princesses, and she wanted me to remember too.)
- A letter opener in the shape of a sword. (Another friend saw the letter opener and thought of me and how I'm always talking about this battle we're in.)
- Several framed pictures and Bible verses given to me by friends to remind me of favorite verses or of who I am in Christ.
- A piece of calligraphy that one of my daughters-in-law gave me; it says, "Love you more." (It's a phrase I've often told my sons and is one that God wants us to hear from Him.)

This cozy place behind a closed door, filled with reminders of God, became a place of worship and peace.

The enemy doesn't give up. He just finds another way to distract us. But God is even more relentless in His pursuit of us.

There is power in God's Word. When we allow God's Word to speak to our lives, it will change us. He's promised that we will be changed just by reading it, meditating on it, and listening to it. As I spent time in God's Word, I was convicted that I had grown lazy and was spending far too many mornings reading what others had written about their relationships with God instead of getting into His Word myself. There is nothing wrong with reading great books. I love reading. Books have spoken powerfully into my life. But they are not a replacement for God's Word. I needed to read it for myself. So I picked up my Bible and began reading again. That summer I started with the book of Mark—all familiar stories. I figured it wouldn't take long to get through the Gospel. As I read, believing God would speak to me, He did. Those familiar stories took on a deeper meaning. By the end of the summer, I was only on Mark 6.

Now some of you may be thinking, *I don't know how to study like that. I pick up my Bible and begin reading, and it's just dry.* Others may be thinking, *I don't understand it.* And still others may be thinking, *They're familiar stories, and I don't see anything new.* Don't give up! Don't let the enemy discourage you. God wants you to understand His Word. He'll help you with this. Talk to Him about it. Pray, and ask Him to speak and give you wisdom as you study. He's promised to give wisdom to anyone who asks (James 1:5). There are also other practical things you can do to make studying the Bible easier.

First, try a few different versions. Read a familiar passage in a number of different translations, and choose the most understandable one. Some people believe that we should only study from certain versions, but if you aren't comprehending what you're reading, it isn't helpful. I study from the New King James Version, but I often compare with other translations when I'm studying to see how other versions have interpreted the original language.

If reading is hard, try an audio version of the Bible. Many apps have the option to listen to God's Word in addition to reading it. Depending on your learning style, you may be able to better understand and comprehend His Word by listening to it.

Try different ways of studying. I love stories, so I enjoy reading through books of the Bible. You can study different topics. I've done word studies, searching for verses on a specific topic. I also enjoy selecting a passage and studying it while reading what others have written about it in commentaries and sermons or discovering what the words meant in the original language. The internet makes searching easy. Websites such as BibleGateway enable you to switch between translations easily and even compare versions side by side.

Talk to others, and see what's helped them go deeper in their studies. For example, if you asked me, I'd tell you that I take a passage or story and just stay with it for several days or a week, reading it over and over. I picture the story unfolding and watch the people and how they would respond in the story. I learn about the times the people were living in and how that impacted the story. Sometimes knowing the thinking of the time gives the story a totally new or deeper meaning than reading it from our worldview.

You don't need to overwhelm yourself as you start. Just pick a version you can easily understand and begin reading, even if it's just for five minutes a day at first. Pray, and ask God to speak to you through His Word. Stop reading when something resonates with you. Meditate on that. Think about it. Write that verse down or turn it into a home screen on your mobile device, and take it with you throughout the day. Let God do His work in you through His Word.

Spend a day

I love my early morning times, but sometimes I need more. So I try to schedule a monthly retreat day—a whole day with just God and me, my Bible, music, and a journal. I get away from the house, where there are too many things that need to be done, and away from the office and its to-do list and interruptions. I typically head to Longwood Gardens because it is a place of such beauty. I walk and listen to music as my heart and mind settle down. Then I find quiet spots to sit and read God's Word or whatever book I'm reading at the time. I journal. My journals are filled with letters to God. My prayers are written out to God as I pray them. I love journaling because it keeps me focused; my mind doesn't wander. And it often causes me to go deeper with God. While we talk about the people for whom I'm praying, we talk about so much more.

You may not be able to imagine spending a whole day of quiet with God. That's OK. Give it a try with just an hour or half a day. Occasionally, I'll take a friend with me. We part ways at the entrance and meet up for lunch in the gardens' restaurant or on the patio. Over lunch, we talk about how God has been speaking to us that morning, what we have been convicted of, and what we're learning. Then we part ways again until it is time to leave, connecting and talking about the afternoon before heading home.

God also gave us the Sabbath as a day to rest in Him and enjoy His company. The Sabbath is also a day to remember that He is the Creator and King of the universe. He is God, and we are not. The world doesn't depend on us. We can stop our efforts for a day, and He will take care of the world. The Sabbath is a weekly reminder that we are not enough but He is enough.

For me, the Sabbath is a day to worship Him in fellowship with others. I'm typically speaking in a different church each week or at a retreat or event. I enjoy sharing God's Word with others and making new friends. The Sabbath often includes a meal with others. When I have the opportunity, I also like getting out for a hike and enjoying nature in the afternoon. And I like spending a quiet afternoon reading a book that will reveal Him in some way. God knew we would need the Sabbath to reset our hearts, rest, forget about work and all the things we need to do, and just focus on Him. On the Sabbath, we can enjoy being with Him and with others who love Him.

But rest doesn't necessarily mean a nap. My husband typically attends our home church on Sabbath, except on the rare occasions when he will join me and share his gift of music with a church to which we've been invited. He's on a team at church that spends one Sabbath afternoon a month hanging out at a children's home, playing games and building relationships with young men who don't have that opportunity in their lives. The people who should have loved them most have wounded them. These young men don't know what healthy relationships with adults look like. This team learns their names, encourages them, and plans events for them. When I have the chance to go with the team, I'm always amazed at my husband's interaction with them and how he truly cares for them. Sabbath is about sharing God's love with others too.

The Sabbath is another opportunity for setting aside a day to enjoy God with others through worship, friendship, nature, and serving.

Life gets busy

Sometimes our commitments slip. Life gets busy. We get distracted. The enemy will persistently try to keep us from spending time with God.

When you realize that you're not hanging out with God or making your relationship with Him a priority, don't allow the enemy to use it as another way to beat yourself up or make you feel like you're not a good enough Christian. Just recommit. Ask God to forgive you for not making the relationship a priority, and ask Him for your focus to get back on track.

God isn't going to beat you up or love you less if you don't make your time with Him a priority. He is going to relentlessly pursue you and convict you to choose the one thing needed—discovering that He is enough. In Him, we find peace, joy, hope, and courage. Spending time with Him isn't about having another thing to do, but it is important because of how it impacts and changes us.

Spending time with Jesus changed Martha's life. She was able to trust Him and find peace when faced with one of the most difficult trials of her life. The enemy could have won that battle easily. He could have convinced her that Jesus didn't care and that was why He didn't show up when Lazarus was dying. He could have continued to build a wall between the sisters. She could have spiraled into despair and hopelessness, thinking God had given up on her and He didn't care that she and her sister were now alone. But the time she spent with Jesus, intentionally choosing to stop and sit at His feet, allowed her to come to know Him in such a way that she didn't doubt His love or care anymore; it also enabled her to ensure that Mary saw Him when she was struggling too.

Time spent with God has changed my life. It slowly transformed the quiet kid who was afraid of everything and everyone, who didn't believe she had much to offer this world, and who figured no one would want to be friends with into a woman who is confident that God loves her and has a plan for her life and who believes that He is working in her and through her. I know my part is to be faithful in growing my relationship with Him and doing what He's called me to do. He'll do the rest. I am not enough, but He is.

Spending time with God will change your life too. One thing is needed; choose it. You will discover that God is enough.

Your story

- How is your relationship with God? How high of a priority is spending time with God? What, if anything, is more important? (You might want to ask God this question and let Him convict you.)
- When or in what ways have you experienced God in a real and life-changing manner?
- Has your time with God ever been more of a *should* than a *need*?
- Has your time with God ever felt like a burden or boring? Do you think

God enjoys the time you spend with Him? Are you really present with Him, or are you just doing what you think you should be doing?

- Do you believe that building a relationship with God is enough? When you read that statement, did you add a few extra things to what you believe you should be doing in order to make yourself be enough?
- Do you believe that God will help you understand His Word and use it to change your daily life and make it practical for today?
- What is the first step you can take in choosing to make time with God the highest priority in your life?

God is enough
God is enough for a life-transforming relationship.

Promise
"Delight yourself also in the LORD, and He shall give you the desires of your heart" (Psalm 37:4).

Prayer
Father God, Ruler of the universe, Creator, Lord, Savior, and Friend, it's beyond comprehension why You want to be friends with us and long to build a relationship with us. Amazingly, You want to speak into our lives and hear all that's on our hearts. Forgive us for letting other things come before You. Forgive us for paying more attention to our social media than to Your Word. Give us a hunger for You. Nothing else will satisfy like You do. God, I want to know You as intimately as a human being can. Work in me. Open my understanding to really see and hear You in Your Word. Help me find that time spent with You is real and practical for my day-to-day life. Help me to find the courage not only to make time with You daily but also to take retreat time to focus on You. Guide me in my Sabbath keeping. Forgive me for the ways I may have made it about the rules instead of truly seeing it as an invitation to choose You and spend time with You. Help me to make the Sabbath a delight for my friends, family, and myself. O God, I love You; help me to love You more. In Jesus' name, amen.

1. Blue Letter Bible, s.v. "*merimnaō*," accessed November 14, 2019, https://www.blueletterbible.org/lang/lexicon/lexicon.cfm?Strongs=G3309&t=NKJV.

2. Blue Letter Bible, s.v. "*thorybazō*," accessed November 14, 2019, https://www.blueletterbible.org/lang/lexicon/lexicon.cfm?Strongs=G5182&t=NKJV.

Chapter 11

The Incredible Gift

It was a phone call that changed my life and scared me to death.

Janet, the leader of the Women's Ministries Department, was moving, and we were looking for her replacement. We talked about numerous names and possibilities for people who could take over Women's Ministries.

She had started Women's Ministries after organizing a retreat and seeing the response of the women. I had attended that first retreat as a young stay-at-home mom getting a weekend away with girlfriends. At one point, my friends chose to go for a walk during a break. I chose to curl up by the fireplace in the lodge where we were staying and spend time with God, read, and journal. That's when I met Janet. She sat down in the chair next to me and started a conversation. I wouldn't learn until years later that a mutual friend had told Janet that she should meet me because she thought God had something for me to do. What I thought was a chance meeting was totally intentional.

I didn't think anything about the conversation until she called the next month and invited me to be part of the team she was forming. I was shocked. Why would she want me to be on the team? I was just a stay-at-home mom with little to offer. Why not ask more important people to be on the team? "Who else is going to be on the team?" I asked, stalling for time as I thought about the opportunity.

"So far, just you and I," she said. Really? Why me? I didn't have training or education. My husband wasn't a pastor. I was a mom to two little boys—a role I loved and enjoyed! But this? Why choose me? In the end, I didn't care why. I knew I wanted to be part of this new ministry. For all of my life, I had wanted to serve God and be involved in a ministry that impacted other people. As a teen, I thought that meant I'd need to marry a pastor. But that didn't happen. As a young mom, I thought maybe God would use me in children's ministries. Women's ministries were just beginning. Was this where God could use me?

For several years, Janet and I worked together with other women partnering with us at different times and in different ways. But Janet and I consistently made up the team. She taught me a lot about prayer, God, and serving. She kept offering new ways for me to serve. She even invited me to speak at events—and that scared me. I was not an up-front person; I was much more comfortable in the background, taking care of the details. But I was beginning to speak frequently at a weekly moms' group and was serving on the leadership team for this outreach to moms, which was sponsored by a local Mennonite church. God seemed to have a plan. I sensed His call to minister to His daughters. I tried to say yes to whatever Janet asked—though not always. (Her version of the story expresses a bit of frustration in my lack of confidence and at my hesitation. Thanks for hanging in there, Janet!)

It was around this time that I wrote my own personal mission statement: "Encouraging, equipping, and challenging women to grow deeply and serve uniquely." (I often use the word *people* in place of "women" these days as God continues to expand my opportunities to serve.)

But now Janet was moving to California. Someone new would need to take over the ministry. I was nervous and excited. I like change. But I hoped the new leader would continue to allow me to serve. I loved this ministry and the women we were serving. Then came the call.

"Tami, Jerry [Janet's husband] is heading to Executive Committee this morning and is presenting a name for the Women's Ministries director position."

"Who is going to be the new leader?" I asked. We had talked about a lot of different people, but I didn't know who Janet and Jerry had chosen.

"You."

"What? You better call him and tell him to stop. I'm not leading! I don't have what it takes. I'll help the new leader, but I can't lead!" I was shocked and afraid. There was no way I had what it took to be a leader. A helper, yes. But leading, organizing events, and finding speakers for retreats? I didn't think so.

"Pray about it, Tami."

I always hated it when Janet told me to pray about something. It meant she was going to get her way because God listened to her. I'm joking! I knew He listened to me just as much as He did her. But the truth was, I didn't want to pray and ask God what He thought because I didn't want Him to tell me to do it. It was too big and too scary.

God and I wrestled as I drove the kids to school that morning. I'm not sure you could call it praying; it was more like telling God all the reasons why I couldn't do the job.

Every time I had a reason for not being enough, God countered with a Bible promise:

"I don't have what it takes."

"I can do all things through Christ who strengthens me" (Philippians 4:13; emphasis added).

"But I'll need to find speakers and locations for retreats. I don't know anybody!"

"My God shall supply all your need according to His riches in glory by Christ Jesus" (Philippians 4:19; emphasis added).

He wasn't letting me off easily, so I made a deal with God. I told Him I'd accept the position if my husband agreed. I knew that Tim liked me to be at home. He didn't really want me to be involved in lots of things. Our sons were just beginning school as our youngest entered first grade that fall. Even with both kids headed to school, Tim was encouraging me to continue staying home and give writing a try. He knew that, too, had always been one of my dreams.

That night Janet and Jerry called and talked to both Tim and me. They explained the position, the expectations, and the small stipend it would pay. That stipend would cover the tuition for the small Christian school the boys were attending. I'll admit that I was shocked when it came time to give an answer. I told Tim, "We need to give an answer to Janet and Jerry this week. It's OK that the answer is no, but they're going to need to know before they leave. What do you think?"

"Well, if you're going to do this, I guess I need to buy you a computer."

It was a moment that changed my life. Saying yes to something bigger than I was—something I knew I wasn't enough for—caused me to depend on God in ways I never had before. I watched God do things in me and through me that had nothing to do with my ability and everything to do with Him. Honestly, if you asked anyone who knew me as a kid or even when I was in high school what they thought, none of them would have believed that I would grow up and travel the country, and even to other countries, to share God on stages in front of hundreds of people. I was the scared kid sitting in the back, sticking to the swings because I was too afraid to play kickball. And then Janet believed in me in a way no one else had before. She believed God had a big plan—a scary plan. (At least, it was scary to me!) Her belief gave me courage, shaky courage, but courage.

The gift of believing God's dream

This wasn't the only time that Janet gave me the gift of believing God had something bigger for me. After settling in California, she invited me to be a speaker at one of her women's retreats. For the first time, I boarded a plane and traveled across the country to stand in front of hundreds of women and share about God.

During the weekend, Janet's prayer partner told me that Janet hadn't been quite sure I would have the courage to get up front and speak once there.

"Then why did she take the risk and pay for me to come?" I asked.

"Because she believed if you did, powerful things would happen."

Her gift of believing that God had plans for my life—plans bigger than anything I hoped for—changed my life. Thirty years later, she continues to dream dreams for me and pray for big things to happen in my life. She encourages my writing. She tells others to invite me to speak or urges them to have me read their manuscripts. She is the first person I knew who believed in me and in God's dream for me.

She hasn't been the only one to give this messy person a chance.

Several years after that scary phone call, I was working part time for the Pennsylvania Conference, assisting the director of the Mission Department and serving as the Women's Ministries director. I had written a half-dozen books and continued to speak at events across the country and in churches in my local community. One day I told Mike, the president, that I would be glad to help write the conference's newsletters during the search for a new Communication director. The previous director had moved across the country. While the conference searched for a new person, the newsletter's deadlines would still need to be met.

"I wish we could hire you for the communication job," he responded.

I laughed. "I can write, but I can't do other things. I don't know anything about websites, and I don't even know how to put a video in a VCR, let alone film and edit a video." (Yes, it was that long ago! Today it's not just websites but the quickly changing digital media field. And our videos are now online and on DVD.)

"You could learn," he replied. "We want someone with your passion for our mission and people."

Years later, Mike and I had a conversation. I told him that hiring me to do communications was the craziest thing he ever did. He laughed and commented that it seemed to work out well for both the conference and for me.

His belief that God could grow me and use me gave me courage. I already knew there was something powerful in stepping into something bigger than you were capable of doing on your own. Mike's belief that I could learn what I didn't know made me want to learn and do the best job I could. It began another crazy journey of growing, learning, and finding new ways of sharing the gospel.

Not just me

Janet and Mike aren't the only ones who have offered this incredible gift of believing that God has a dream for us. Samuel offered this blessing to David. We find the story in 1 Samuel 16. God sent Samuel to Bethlehem, which is about five miles south of Jerusalem. Samuel's job was to anoint the next king. He invited Jesse and his sons to attend the sacrifice as God instructed. Jesse brought his sons, but not all of them. David was out watching their sheep. As David was the youngest, Jesse probably didn't even give David a thought. He wasn't important enough.

When Samuel met Eliab, Jesse's oldest son, Samuel thought he looked like king material. After all, he was the oldest, and the oldest son was the most important. But God said, No, not him. "Do not look at his appearance or at his physical stature, because I have refused him. For the LORD does not see as man sees; for man looks at the outward appearance, but the LORD looks at the heart" (verse 7).

Eliab might have looked like he had what it took to be king, but God hadn't chosen him. They went through all of Jesse's sons, and not one king was among them. Samuel probably wondered what was going on. God had said He was calling one of Jesse's sons, and then He didn't choose any of them. Scratching his head, he asked Jesse, "Are these all of your sons?"

That's when Jesse tells him about David. They stop the meal and wait for someone to go get David. Despite the fact that David was the youngest and had almost been forgotten by his father, Samuel believes in God's dream for him. He anoints David and believes that God has called him to be king.

The king thing doesn't happen right away. There's already a king on the throne.

But King Saul is struggling. The Bible says, "A distressing spirit from the LORD troubled him" (verse 14). God may have been convicting Saul because he was no longer listening to God. The servants suggest that music might soothe his spirit, so they call for a musician. Guess who? David. He happens to be not only a shepherd but also a gifted musician. Whenever David would play music, Saul's spirit would calm, and he would feel better.

But life doesn't calm down. In 1 Samuel 17, Saul and his army head off to war against the Philistines. That's where they encounter Goliath—a giant who taunts the Israelites day and night. Every day God's army suited up for battle and then just stood there, too afraid to fight. Goliath challenged them every morning and evening for forty days. When David shows up to see how things are going, he can't believe that they're letting Goliath get away with defying God in that way. He gathers a few stones and his sling and slays the giant. The Philistines flee. Saul's men gain courage and pursue the fleeing enemy, killing them and plundering what they leave behind. Victory!

There was a problem with the celebration for Saul though. People were singing about David, and that made Saul angry. And it made him want to kill David. He didn't want people to like David better, and he definitely wasn't going to step aside and let David be king. He begins to pursue David to destroy him.

Many years pass before David becomes king. He spends his life on the run, hiding from a king who wants him dead. It had to be hard. Did he ever doubt God's call for his life?

Jonathan doesn't doubt. He believes God has called David to be king. The thing is, Jonathan is next in line for the throne. He should be the king after his father, Saul. But he sees God at work and believes God's dream for David. He promises David his friendship and support. Then he takes off his robe and gives it to David. He gives David his armor, including his sword and bow and belt. He is symbolically showing his belief in God's dream for David. David will be king one day, not Jonathan.

Later he speaks this belief.

David is hiding in the wilderness. Saul is relentlessly hunting David in order to kill him. David is struggling. He's hiding deep in the woods. He must be wondering whether God's call is real; if it is, why is it taking so long? He's tired of running and hiding and doubting that he will ever be king. Even though Saul can't find him, Jonathan does. "Then Jonathan, Saul's son, arose and went to David in the woods and strengthened his hand in God. And he said to him, 'Do not fear, for the hand of Saul my father shall not find you. You shall be king over Israel, and I shall be next to you. Even my father Saul knows that' " (1 Samuel 23:16, 17).

I love the phrase "strengthened his hand in God." Jonathan sought out David to encourage him and give him the strength to keep trusting God. He affirms that David will be king one day. Even though most people assume that Jonathan will rule after his father, Jonathan pledges that he will support David.

What an incredible gift it is to believe God's dream for another person and not compare or compete—just encourage, affirm, strengthen, and promise to be right there, helping! Although many years will pass from the anointing in Bethlehem until David takes the throne, God keeps sending people who believe His calling for David's life, and they affirm and encourage him.

There is at least one more person who believes in God's dream for David. This time, it's a woman.

David and his men are still on the run. David hears that Nabal, a rich man with three thousand sheep and a thousand goats, is shearing his sheep. David sends ten of his men to go and ask for a gift. They've protected Nabal's shepherds, and they feel as though they deserve a reward. Nabal has plenty, and it's a feast day. So why wouldn't he share? (1 Samuel 25).

Nabal is not in a generous mood. He acts like he doesn't have a clue who David is and refuses to send him anything. He insults David as if he's an outlaw or a runaway servant.

This doesn't go over well with David. He's ready for a fight and tells his guys to grab their swords.

Enter Abigail. She's actually pushed into the story. A servant saw how Nabal responded to David's men. He saw David's men protect Nabal's shepherds and their flocks. He recognizes that something bad is about to happen. He goes to Abigail and asks her to do something. The Bible tells us that Abigail is "a woman of good understanding and beautiful appearance" (verse 3). She's smart. The young man knows she'll figure out what to do. Maybe the servants have previously needed to ask Abigail to save the day.

Abigail quickly goes into action. Packing up a feast on the backs of donkeys, she rides out, without Nabal's knowledge, to head David off. When she sees David, she falls at his feet and addresses him as lord. She shows respect where Nabal insults. She reminds David that God promises he will be king. She reminds him of how God has protected him. God convicts David and keeps him from destroying Nabal. Abigail gives David the incredible gift of believing in God's dream for him, affirming him in it, and challenging him not to mess it up.

Samuel plants the dream.

Jonathan reaffirms the dream when David is discouraged.

Abigail reminds David of the dream and challenges him not to do anything that would hurt God's plan.

Each person encouraged David. Each one gave him the strength and the hope to wait on God—an incredible gift.

The dreamers in your life

Who are the dreamers in your life? Who has come alongside you and encouraged what God is doing in you and through you? Who has given you opportunities to use your talents?

Your dreamers' gifts to you may not be quite as big as Janet's or Mike's were to me, but they are there. As I read over this chapter, I'm reminded that Marilee, who is a friend, encouraged Janet to seek me out and get to know me because she believed God had something for me to do. I remember that my husband encouraged me to stay home and pursue my dream of writing when I could have gone to work part time and earned more money than writing brought in. But there have been others who have spoken quietly into my life. My neighbor Elsie started the moms' group at her church and invited me to attend. Then she asked me to be the one community member on the leadership team and also invited me to speak. I don't remember how that ever happened! But it was where I began to speak. All of my early books came from talks I shared at that group. There also was Ray, who could have agreed that Mike's decision was crazy and who could have chosen a more experienced Communication director when he became president. But Ray continued to give me opportunities to learn and grow and made me feel like I was a part of the team.

Even back in high school, there was the teacher who wrote affirming notes on my writing assignments—even encouraging me to submit one to a magazine. There was the English teacher who told me I had a great speaking voice on the one and only day I was convinced to give the morning announcements over the intercom at school. (I shook the whole time I spoke into the microphone behind a soundboard in an office. No one could see me, but I was scared silly. I was never willing to do it again despite the teacher's encouraging words.)

Maybe you can quickly identify people who believed in you and encouraged you: a teacher, a parent, a friend, or even a stranger. For many, it may be harder. Ask God to help you see the people He's sent your way to encourage and affirm His dreams for you. It may be hard. Too often, when we struggle with how we see ourselves and believe that we're not enough or don't have anything special to offer, we dismiss compliments and affirmations and tell ourselves why they're not true.

Identifying God's call

It's important to look for the areas in which people are affirming that God is using us or in which He has equipped us. These are opportunities to discover what He's called us to do. There's no way I would be leading or speaking today if others hadn't affirmed these areas in my life. I would never have believed it for myself. Yet as I look back through my life, I can see that writing and speaking are the areas people have been affirming all the way back to when I was a little girl.

God has written your story. He has a role for you to play—a way to change your world—for the people you love and the people you don't know yet. He's given you specific talents and abilities, and He will affirm you in these areas. He will bring people who will encourage you in them. These people will tell you how you're making a difference in their lives. It may be a simple thank-you note or a word of encouragement in passing. There may be people who will speak in bigger ways, like Janet has for me, or invite you to do something that you may not believe you're capable of doing. Pray about it. Consider that God may have something new for you.

If you struggle to believe that you have anything to offer or think that you can't make a difference, stop and look for the ways people have affirmed you. Negative, critical words always seem louder and are easier to remember, but other words are there. Ask God to help you remember and hear the words of encouragement and believe them. Then step out in faith in these areas, asking God to give you opportunities to share your gift. Begin in simple ways. Before I began writing books, I wrote notes of encouragement to people. Despite having opportunities to preach and speak now, I'm intentional about sharing words of encouragement with people, even strangers, throughout the day. I believe the small things we do will have a larger impact than we believe. A word of encouragement at just the right time may be more life changing than a sermon. A meal dropped off during a crazy time can speak hope and help. An invitation to lunch may help someone else begin to think that people do see him or her and might just want to be a friend.

You, my friend, were created on purpose. God will give you opportunities and send people who encourage you. Maybe those opportunities seem a bit crazy, but God loves to invite us into places where, on our own, we're not enough. But with Him, amazing things can happen.

A gift you want to share

The gifts others have spoken into my life have given me courage and helped me to identify my God-given abilities. And others have offered me opportunities to use these gifts. They were catalysts for how God has moved and worked in my life. This has been an incredible blessing that I want to offer others. When you've experienced it, you want others to experience it as well. You want to pay it forward and help others find courage and discover what God has equipped them to do.

It takes courage to offer this gift, especially if you're encouraging people with abilities similar to yours. Sometimes we have a scarcity mind-set. We think if others do what we're doing, then there won't be enough opportunities for us both. (This is not true. When God gifts, He brings you to serve in the ways and places that He has for you.) And of course, there's that problem with comparing and competing. When we're not sure we're enough or are good enough or whatever, we tend to compare how we're doing with others. Without even thinking about it, we can fall into competing—trying to do something better.

The enemy loves that trick. If he can get us to compare and compete with others, then we won't truly trust God or connect with each other. But avoiding this trick requires feeling secure in who you are in Christ. And this goes back to the one thing needed. When we make a relationship with God the top priority in our lives and begin discovering who we are in Him and who He is, we can trust Him with the details of our lives and rest secure that we are where we need to be. This gives us the freedom to encourage others and truly be happy for them when they succeed and not let their accomplishments make us feel less than.

This concept is one of the powerful parts of Jonathan's story. He didn't compare himself to or compete against David. He didn't see David as a threat. He was secure in who he was and trusted God. He didn't need to be king in order to prove himself or find his value. He was perfectly content supporting David since that is who God chose. He wanted God's will, even though it put him at odds with his dad—and even though it meant that he wouldn't be king.

I want to be like Jonathan. I want to trust God enough to encourage others, even when they do what I do or, harder still, get the opportunity that I want. I want to offer the incredible gift of speaking belief into other people's lives and giving them the courage to believe God has a plan. And when I have the opportunity, I want to invite people into places where they can use their abilities for Him, even when it's scary or they wonder whether they have what it takes. I want to be the person that cheers them on. I look for opportunities to encourage, affirm, and dream for others every day. I do this not just in the lives of adults and friends but also in the lives of young women, teens, and girls.

My friend Denise tells people that I did this for her. I called her out of the blue one day and asked her to present a seminar at a women's retreat that I was organizing. Really, it was our mutual friend Linda who believed in her; I didn't even know her. But Linda had recommended her, and I trusted Linda. So I called. Denise has been speaking and preaching ever since. I've enjoyed watching God work in and through Denise and give her a powerful ministry that helps women who are hurting. Doing similar things with totally different styles has given us a unique bond. Instead of competing, we are able to be truly excited for each other as God leads and opens up opportunities. We enjoy speaking together, too, even though we do push each other out of our comfort zones because of our different styles. It has been a blessing to walk together on this journey instead of competing with each other. The enemy does tempt us to do that. I remember someone coming to me once and telling me that her group had just invited Denise to speak at its next event. She said, "We've invited Denise because she's the complete package. She can speak and sing." It really felt like this person emphasized the words *complete* and *and*. For a moment, my heart began the journey to think, *I'm not enough. I can't sing and speak.* But I caught the enemy in action. I smiled and told the woman that her group would love Denise. I knew I didn't need to be everything or do everything. God has plenty for me.

On the days when my trust in God is strong and I'm secure in Him, I can truly encourage and affirm others without reservation. I can walk into a room filled with beautiful, talented women and not feel less than or want to shrink into the background. Instead, I engage in conversation, speak words of encouragement, and just be me, knowing that God loves me and makes me enough. I remind myself that in the room are women just like me, struggling with how they see themselves and how they see God. They wonder whether they're enough and sometimes doubt that God can use them. They might need Jonathans in their lives who will strengthen their hand in God. I want to be that person for others: reaffirming God's love and call, offering to be right there with them, cheering them on, and reminding them that God's got them and their lives.

Your story

- Who has God brought into your life to speak courage to His dreams for you? If you can't think of anyone, pray and ask God to open your eyes to the ways people have believed in you.
- Who has offered you opportunities that were bigger than you could accomplish on your own and believed they were possible with God?
- Are there specific areas of your life where people keep affirming and encouraging you? Are you using these areas or abilities to help others in their journey to know God more? If not, why not? Do you still doubt or struggle to believe that God would really use you?
- Who are you offering this incredible gift to?

God is enough

God is enough to write a bigger story than you can imagine and send people who believe in you and Him.

Promise

" 'For I know the plans I have for you,' declares the Lord, 'plans to prosper you and not to harm you, plans to give you hope and a future' " (Jeremiah 29:11, NIV).

Prayer

O Lord, You know me. You have created me to be me and have written my story in Your book. You have plans for me, plans that bring hope and courage. Thank You for loving me so much! You know how I wrestle and doubt. Sometimes I wonder whether You really have a plan for me. Encourage me. Help me to discover and grow in Your plans. Thank You for sending people to affirm and encourage me; these are people who dream Your dreams for me and invite me to take that next step. Father, You know how easy it is for me to focus on the negative, critical words spoken to and about me. I surrender them to You. Help me to lay them down at Your feet and let them go. God, don't let them have any authority over my life or identity. Give me the courage to believe Your words and to see and hear the ways that You are encouraging, affirming, guiding, and using me. Help me to trust You so much that I don't compare or compete with others but encourage them in Your plan for their lives, knowing that even if we're doing the same things, You have opportunities for both of us. God, use me to encourage others in this journey too. Help me strengthen their hand in Yours. In Jesus' name, amen.

Chapter 12

Stepping Into God's Big Things

’ll never forget her face. She was standing in the back of the room, just glowing with joy and peace that was visible. "I gave my life to Jesus," she exclaimed excitedly when I approached. She told me how a friend had asked her that week to attend this women's retreat. She had come at the last minute and discovered a God who loved her.

It was the first time I offered an invitation at the end of one of my presentations—actually, two invitations. The first was to those who already knew and loved God but realized their need to go deeper and make a relationship with Him a priority in their lives. Nearly half the room came forward to pray and commit themselves. The second invitation was to those who had never surrendered their lives. Almost a dozen women responded; they were greeted by members of the leadership team who prayed with them while tears flowed. My own tears streamed down my face as I stood on the stage, watching and waiting to end the time with prayer.

I stood in awe of this amazing God who allowed me to be part of what He was doing in these women's lives. I knew it wasn't about me. I had shown up and been faithful to what He asked me to do. He was already at work in their lives—already drawing them and preparing them for this moment.

It was the first but not the last time I watched people commit their lives to Christ or commit to going deeper. At one retreat, two women who came forward were baptized. Afterward, the friends of one came to me excitedly. "We never thought we'd see this day! She's been coming with us for years but has never seemed interested in anything more than the weekend!"

Janet's scary phone call changed my life and changed me. I reluctantly said yes and stepped into an adventure that was bigger than anything I could have done on my own. I knew I wasn't enough; I wasn't experienced enough or educated enough or—I'm not even sure of all the "not enoughs" I felt at the time. But instead of allowing the enemy to use my not enoughness to keep me from trying, those "not enoughs" caused me to depend on God instead of on myself.

One of the life-changing lessons I've learned in my journey is that when we take a risk, swallow our fear, and step out into something bigger than we are capable of on our own, God is enough. He does amazing things in us and through us. I've discovered God is bigger than my insecurities and not enoughness and any of the other ways I've limited Him. I once read a thought from a Bible study that really impacted me. The authors wrote, "When you believe that nothing consequential can happen through you, you have said more about your belief in God than you have indicated about yourself."[1]

Did that hit you like it did me?

"When you believe that nothing consequential can happen through you . . ." When you believe that you're not enough, you doubt God's Word. When you believe that you have nothing to offer the world, you doubt God's work in your life. When you believe that you'll never impact the world around you, you doubt God's ability to use you for His mission.

"You have said more about your belief in God than you have indicated about yourself." Wait. Weren't we talking about *our* not enoughness? How does this reveal anything about our beliefs about God? We know *He's* enough. We are the problem, right?

Think about it. When we say we have nothing to offer, we're calling God a liar. He's promised in His Word that the Spirit has chosen gifts for each of us, and these gifts are given so that we can impact the church and those who don't know God yet (1 Corinthians 12). When we say we can't, we're saying that God isn't big enough to work through us. Really? Do we really think we're too big of a problem for the God who created the entire universe, calms storms with just a word, heals, raises people from the dead, and conquered sin for eternity?

God is bigger than our failures. He is bigger than our insecurities and lack of confidence. He is bigger than our fears. There is nothing impossible for Him. He spoke through Moses, who had slow speech. He worked through Jacob, who was a liar and manipulator. He called David a man after His own heart even after David had an affair, had the woman's husband killed, and then married her. And those are just a small, random sampling of God's redemption stories.

When God calls us to something bigger than we are capable of doing, He knows. He knows we're not capable on our own. He is inviting us to discover more of who we are and who He is. Picture Him standing there, hand extended, inviting you to something that will change your life.

Trusting Him

In the beginning, I struggled and beat myself up. Even though I was saying yes to the opportunities God was sending my way, I was still too focused on myself and my abilities—or my lack of abilities. I'd head to a church or retreat to speak and be so nervous, so sure that I couldn't do it and shouldn't do it, that I would promise myself I'd never say yes again. Afterward, on the drive home, I would beat myself up. I should have said this. I shouldn't have said that. Why was I so animated? I should be calmer. On one car ride home, God interrupted one of these battles.

"Did you pray about this?"

I had prayed a lot.

"Did you ask Me to do what I wanted to do?"

Yes. I had begged God to show up and speak into hearts, for it to be Him and not me.

"Do you trust Me that I did what I wanted, no matter how you think it went?"

That. Stopped. Me. In. My. Tracks. That afternoon was a turning point for me. I realized that my role in this adventure was to do what God asked me to do: pray, study, prepare, go, and share what He had taught me and done in my life. The rest was up to Him. The results are His part. How people respond and what they think are His responsibility. I can't change people. I can only do what He's asked me to do. He alone can change hearts, impact people, and draw them to Himself. Realizing this brought freedom and peace. It gave me the courage to do what He's called me to do, believing that He will show up and accomplish whatever it is that He wants. I've learned to stop focusing on my not enoughness and just trust Him.

I now go, expecting God to work. The results aren't because of me: I know the truth about myself; I'm not enough. I'm a messy person and a sinner. I struggle with doubt. I wrestle with fear. I look in the mirror and am not always nice to myself. But I love God and truly desire for Him to be not just Savior but Lord of my life. I long for Him to use me however He desires. I believe He uses us not because we're enough but because He is. He knows that when we're willing to swallow our fears and our not enoughness, take His hand, and step into the way-too-big adventure He's called us to, it will change us and grow us. It will deepen our faith and trust. It will help us to discover new things about ourselves and about Him.

Discovering purpose and passion

Esther didn't want to step into anything bigger than she was. She was content to live a quiet life, hiding who she really was from the world around her. She wanted to blend in, not stand out. She was a Jew living in Persia. Her people had been taken into captivity years before. Eventually, they were allowed to return to Jerusalem, but many, like Esther's family, had grown comfortable in Persia. They chose to stay instead of going back to the land God had given them and reclaiming their lives as His people. They chose comfort over the hard journey of returning and rebuilding.[2]

Esther is an orphan living with her cousin Mordecai. Her real name is Hadassah, but she is known by her Persian name, which is another way of blending in. Esther learned at a young age to hide who she really is. Throughout her story in the Old Testament book that bears her name, her cousin tells her not to reveal who she really is. So she hides the fact that she is a Jew. It has to make her feel like she isn't enough, and she fears what could happen if people discover who she really is.

One day she is taken from her home, whether she likes it or not, to prepare for one night with the king. Hundreds of beautiful young virgins, meaning they'd be in their early teens, are taken into another form of captivity. For a year, Esther is given beauty treatments. Oils and lotions soften her skin. She is given clothes that accent her beauty. She is pampered and has servants to care for her. She is already beautiful—inside and out. We know this because the Bible tells us she is lovely and beautiful and also because of the way people respond to her. Hegai, the eunuch who is in charge of the young women, favors her. She isn't demanding. She is obedient and easily follows all that he asks. So he gives her the best room, the best servants, and extra beauty treatments.

After a year of these beauty treatments—and enough time has passed to ensure that the young woman is not pregnant—each girl spends a night with the king. This will be their first, and possibly last, encounter with a man. They will go to the king in the evening, and the next morning they move into the house with other women who have spent a night with the king and now just live in the house, cared for, but with no real purpose or future. They have no home of their own, no children unless they happen to get pregnant during that one night, and no one to love them and share their lives. A house filled with women who were, in essence, not enough for the king couldn't be a very happy place to live. Think of all the ways that would impact each woman: they would compare, compete, and struggle to find purpose while believing they have none.

When Esther's time to go to the king arrives, she can take anything she wants. She understands that Hegai knows the king best, so she takes only what he advises. Her beauty and grace capture the king's attention, and he chooses her to be queen. Instead of moving in with the other women, she moves into the queen's area of the palace. But she's still hiding a secret while keeping up appearances, doing what is expected, trying to please.

One day she hears that her cousin is hanging out at the king's gate in sackcloth and ashes, crying out loudly and bitterly. He is *not* keeping up appearances. Instead of sending out a messenger to find out what's happening, she sends him clothes and tells the servants to take away his sackcloth. Mordecai had taught her well to hide and look good on the outside, no matter what was on the inside. She wants him to quickly look the part of a respectable gatekeeper again. But he refuses. This time she sends a servant to find out why, and his response frightens her.

Suddenly, Mordecai wants her not only to reveal who she really is but break the rules and go to the king uninvited. Esther does not want to do it. She's crafted her life around hiding, keeping the rules, being the good girl, and trying to be the good-enough girl. She says no.

Her cousin's words in return push her to do something bigger than she can on her own: go to the king uninvited and plead for her people—people she has never claimed before—and for a God whom she may or may not have worshiped before. Mordecai challenges her, "Yet who knows whether you have come to the kingdom for such a time as this?" (Esther 4:14).

Esther swallows her fears and chooses to step into the room with the king uninvited, regardless of what happens, and discovers her purpose and passion. As she steps up, God moves in powerful ways. The enemy is defeated. The king is delighted. Mordecai is elevated to a higher position. And Esther's story is included in God's Word.

Esther doesn't do it alone. Mordecai challenges her as Janet did me. Esther asks the Jews to pray for her and gathers her group of girls and fasts and prays. I can't even tell you what it has done for me to have friends who have rallied, prayed for me, and cheered me on. Just as I was writing Esther's story, a friend called and prayed for me, for this book, and for the words. Others have emailed or texted to let me know that they're praying. My friend Kathleen is listening to each chapter as I finish it and read it to her through the Marco Polo app. Her words have encouraged me to keep writing and keep stepping into what God has called me to do.

Like Esther, when we find the courage to do the things that are so big we can't do them on our own, we will discover our purpose and passion. And we will learn more about ourselves and about God. As I have written, preached, and worked in ministry for the last thirty years, I have experienced God in ways that I never would have otherwise. That young mom who longed to make an impact but was unsure how God wanted to use her discovered His call to care for His girls. Esther found that when she stopped hiding who she was, trusted God, and stepped into His big plan for her, she was called at that moment to save her people.

It's hard. Submitting that first manuscript was scary—even submitting this one was. What if people don't like it? What if it's not good enough? What if I'm not enough? But what if it is what God is calling you to do? What if He wants you to let go and do something you cannot succeed at without Him so that you discover Him and that He is enough? What if this moment, this opportunity in front of you, is part of what God created you to do?

Don't forget the small things

There's a quote—really part of a quote—on the letter board in my kitchen right now. It's attributed to Eleanor Roosevelt, although she didn't really say it. Regardless of who originally said it, it's good advice. "Do one thing every day that scares you. Those small things that make us uncomfortable help us build the courage to do the work we do."

I'll tweak that a bit: "Do one thing with God each day that is bigger than you can do on your own. Even the smallest step out in faith will give you the courage to trust God more and do what He's created you to do."

The too-big thing God may be calling you to step into may not be a ministry or job. It may not be to get up front and speak or get behind a computer and write. It may be ordinary or small things done every day. But when it is done with God, it will make a huge impact in your life and the life of others.

- Try a new activity that you might not be good at.
- Reach out in friendship to someone whom you'd love to get to know but

aren't sure he or she would want to get to know you, or you fear may be too busy or too "together" to be your friend.

- Speak up and share your thoughts in a small group, Bible study, meeting at work, or around the table with friends.
- Take a new class that interests you.
- Pursue your degree.
- Join a new group: a book club, Bible study, moms' time-out, neighbors' gathering, or running club.
- Hire a fitness trainer, and take your exercise to the next level.
- Sign up for a 5K or a marathon.
- Share your story—even just part of it—with others when God prompts.
- Write an encouraging note to someone.
- Take a meal to a new mom, new neighbor, or someone you know who is going through a tough time.
- Volunteer at your kids' school, in your community, or at a local retirement center.
- Apply for that job you want but aren't sure you're ready for.
- Buy a bunch of flowers at the grocery store, and then pray and give them to strangers.
- Pray regularly for one of the "hard" people in your life—the person you want to avoid because he or she is difficult or has hurt you.

Even if you try something and decide you're just not into it after all or you don't succeed at it, the act of stepping out, trusting God, and swallowing the fear will give you the courage to try again. And you just might discover something new that you do enjoy. In any case, you'll learn new things about yourself, and if you trust God to give you courage and help you, you'll discover new things about God. You'll discover that no matter how insufficient you may be, God is enough.

A note about ministry

Since we're talking about finding your purpose and passion, I just want to add a note about ministry. Sometimes we think that ministry means preaching, writing, leading, or singing. But it's so much more than those things. Ministry is whatever and however God calls you to impact the world.

- Parenting is a huge ministry.
- Loving your spouse well, helping your spouse to be the person God created him or her to be, cheering your spouse on, and gently asking the tough questions that challenge him or her is a ministry.
- Teaching the kids' classes at church is a ministry.
- Opening your home to a small group is a ministry.
- Writing a note of encouragement is a ministry.

- Helping others in practical ways is a ministry.
- Listening is a ministry.
- Creating beauty for people to enjoy, whether through art, gardening, decorating, or something else, is a ministry.

Whenever we use our time, talents, and passions for God, it's ministry.

Serving God doesn't just happen on a platform. It happens in the kitchen, on the train, or in the break room at work. It happens while going for a walk in your neighborhood or listening to a friend at your local café.

Ministry happens any time you use your unique gifts and passions to meet a need in the life of a person, whether young or old, someone you know or a complete stranger.

The enemy doesn't want any of this to happen. He doesn't want you to use your gifts and passions for God. He doesn't want you to make an impact on people and bring them courage, hope, and a deeper experience with God and His love. He will always attempt to take you out, discourage you, and cause you to believe that what you are doing isn't enough, isn't needed, or isn't big enough to make a difference. He doesn't want you to make an impact in the way God desires. And he is a liar. Don't listen to him. Listen instead to the One who loves you more than you've ever been loved—the One who believes you can impact others and make a difference because He created you to do that very thing for such a time as this.

It's an adventure you don't want to miss

I've often told my sons, "God has an adventure for you, and you don't want to miss it." My friend, it's true for you too. He has a plan for you, and you don't want to miss it. He has big plans and small, daily plans—plans that will give you hope and courage as you walk through them.

There have been a lot of things I haven't tried because I didn't want to fail or I feared that I couldn't do them perfectly or I would look silly. I've missed out on fun things, life-changing things, and things that would have stretched me and grown me in new ways. But I'm learning to let go of the fear and just try. Whether it's taking voice lessons or a painting class, hiring a trainer to help me figure out how to use the weights at the gym, or just asking someone new whether she'd like to have lunch, I'm growing and enjoying something new with each step. I'm becoming braver and more like the woman God created me to be.

Even the littlest acts of stepping out of my fear and taking the risk of not doing something well bring me more confidence and courage.

Recently, I was in the Governor's Palace at Colonial Williamsburg, which is a living-history museum in Virginia, when they were getting ready for a ball. "George Washington" was looking for someone to take dance lessons with him. He asked a couple of women who all said no and laughed. They were clearly uncomfortable with making a fool of themselves in front of the gathering of tourists. When he asked me, I swallowed that fear and said yes. And I did not dance perfectly! I looked behind me when I was walking backward, which the dance instructor told me (in front of everyone in a very smug, disgusted voice) was a huge no-no. I guess it was better to back into someone than to look behind you. But it was fun. We laughed. I tried something silly and enjoyed it, and I can now say I danced with "George Washington." It was a small thing, but just one more time I didn't let the enemy win.

We can't let the enemy win and keep us from what God wants for us. He longs to devour us and take us out and keep us from doing and being who God created us to be. As I've said before, sometimes his attack is the greatest just before God is going to use us in a big way or call us to the next step in His plan. The enemy wants to thwart that. Don't let him win.

Swallow your fear and all of your "not enoughs," grab God's hand, ask a friend to pray, and step into things bigger than you. Focus on God and all He is able to do and all that He's promised to do. You don't want to miss what will happen next.

Your story
- What are you afraid of? What have you been too scared to do? Are these big or little things?
- Have there been times when you swallowed your fear and tried something that was too big for you to do on your own without God? What was that like?
- Are there things right now that you're afraid to do, but God is inviting you to step into? What's the worst thing that could happen if you try? What's the best thing that could happen if you try?
- What's one small, courageous thing you could do this week?
- How do you believe God wants you to use your talents and passion to meet a need in someone's life?

God is enough
God is enough to conquer your fears and do big things through you.

Promise
"For God has not given us a spirit of fear, but of power and of love and of a sound mind" (2 Timothy 1:7).

Prayer
Creator God, Warrior, and Conqueror, You are the One who speaks peace, calms storms, and casts out fear. You are a God who calls us to big things. You've created us uniquely and intentionally and then placed us at this moment and in these places to be a part of Your bigger plan. Forgive us for being afraid, for hiding who we really are, and for not wanting to take risks or step out in faith and just wanting to

stay comfortable. Give us Your courage and boldness to do what You invite us to do—big things and small things. Help us to swallow our fear, take Your hand, and watch You do things in and through us that we never thought possible. Father, keep our eyes open to the times when we can walk alongside our friends and pray for them to be courageous and live the life You've created them to live. Let us also be warriors, fighting for those we love, encouraging them to trust You, and believing that You've created each of us for things bigger than we can do alone. We love You. Don't let us miss the adventure. In Jesus' name, amen.

1. Henry T. Blackaby, Richard Blackaby, and Claude King, *Experiencing God*, rev. and expanded ed. (Nashville, TN: B&H Publishing, 2008), 47.

2. See Ellen G. White, *Prophets and Kings* (Mountain View, CA: Pacific Press®, 1917), 598.

Chapter 13

The Story We Tell Ourselves

t's ironic that this is the chapter I need to write next as I sit down at the computer today. Yesterday was a big, important family gathering. I'm not sure why, but family gatherings are often where I struggle the most. I can walk into a room filled with hundreds of women with confidence and strength, believing God loves me and has a purpose for my life. I feel no comparison or competition; I just sincerely want to care, listen, make friends, and encourage. But walking into family events brings out the old insecurities that wreak a bit of havoc on my heart. I'm a bit on edge and worry about what others are thinking and how they'll respond to me. I guess with family you've learned what to expect: the complainers; the grouches; the quiet-in-the-corner ones; the big, filling-the-room attention seekers; and the people for whom you are just never enough. You tend to know from experience how people are going to respond and what they're going to say.

So yesterday was a battle. I stressed about what to wear. I worked extra hard to tame my easily frizzy hair. I felt a bit disconnected. Small talk is hard for introverts, and there was a lot of opportunity for small talk but not many chances for real conversation. I admit that I attempted to avoid the complainers and grouches. I tried to make sure to connect with various family members whom I hadn't seen in a while. And I tried to remember to smile. (I get so focused that I don't smile—not because I'm not happy but because I'm focused and thinking.) It was one of those days when you needed a girlfriend by your side to remind you that God loves you and you have value.

This morning as the dust settles and people head home, I feel discouraged. Scanning the photos of the day, I start to beat myself up for not being thin enough or pretty enough. Thinking back over conversations, I wish I had said this or that, talked to this person, and connected with that one. The enemy reminds me that I'm just not good at social events. I'm not engaging enough. I don't converse on enough different topics. If I don't battle back, I'll spiral down into thinking that people don't enjoy hanging out with me and they would rather be with someone else. Lord, help me!

It's a story we've learned

Family gatherings and class reunions are moments when the past and present collide. Old stories (or maybe current stories) come rushing back to our memories like an old song we haven't heard since our teen years, but the minute we hear it, we're singing along, remembering every word.

For most of us, childhood is where the story of not being enough began. As little girls and especially as teens, we heard the message loud and clear: we are not enough:

- not good enough
- not smart enough
- not quiet enough
- not talkative enough
- not pretty enough
- not thin enough
- not athletic enough
- not (fill in the blank) enough

And the story is repeated over and over from different sources and with different variations. But typically, we have a place in our heart that is especially wounded. This area is where we feel the most like we are not enough. It becomes the story we live and tell ourselves. It becomes our truth. We've believed it for so long that it feels like the truth of who we are. We don't even attempt to question it.

We didn't know there was an enemy out to destroy us when we were little girls. We didn't know that we lived in a battleground. We believed the lies about ourselves and our lives because we didn't know better. But now we're grown up, and it's time to tell ourselves a new story.

Time to learn a new story

As I mentioned in chapter 2, the woman with the issue of blood was told she was unclean (Mark 5). It was the rule of the day: a woman was unclean while she had her period. After seven days, she could make an offering and be good to go. Only this woman's bleeding never stopped. The story she was told grew. Many would tell her it was her fault. She must have done something horrible, and now God was punishing her. God cursed her. He didn't love her. He didn't want her. I'm sure she prayed and prayed for healing, begging God to make it stop. As weeks, then months, and finally years passed, her unanswered prayers spoke to the story she told herself. She was not good enough for God to heal.

Most likely, her family and friends were sympathetic in the beginning, then they eventually distanced themselves. Who wants to hang around someone whom God has obviously cursed and is considered unclean by society? Their distance and departure from her life brought loneliness. They added to the story that she wasn't good enough—not enough for people to stick it out with her, be her friend, and encourage her. They certainly weren't allowed to hug her, or they'd become unclean. It must have been incredibly painful to know that everything and anyone she touched became unclean because of her.

She spent her money, trying to get better but only grew worse. She sold items from her home and went to anyone, anywhere, in an attempt to find healing. But no one could make her well. The bleeding and fatigue worsened. She was physically, emotionally, mentally, and spiritually depleted.

Then she began to tell herself a new story (verse 28). "If only I can get to Jesus."

She'd heard the stories. Maybe she'd witnessed His miracles or heard Him teach. But somehow, she'd learned about Jesus and began believing that if she could just get to Him, she'd be made well. The new story gave her courage, hope, and boldness. Despite the physical fatigue and weakness the bleeding must have brought, she was on her feet and attempting to push through the crowd, focused on getting to Jesus. Her belief and faith grew as she repeated this new story to herself over and over: "Jesus can heal me."

Telling a new story changed everything. The woman found healing, and not just physically. Jesus wouldn't let her go until He had spoken into every area of her life.

Friends, we need to tell ourselves a new story. Stop rehearsing the old "not-enough" words we use to beat ourselves up. It's time to stop living in defeat and instead grow into the women God designed us to be and created in His image for this moment in time. It's time we quit telling ourselves we don't have what it takes and start believing God does. It's time to come out of hiding, say goodbye to our fears, and start living like we believe God loves us.

Every thought captive

Our inner dialogue needs to change. We need to stop repeating the old stories every time we look in the mirror, fail at something, don't get invited or included, awkwardly trip over nothing, burn dinner, or whatever sends our brains down the old, familiar defeating-and-discouraging pathways of not being enough. Literally telling ourselves new stories will physically rewire our thinking, creating new paths for our thoughts and a new view of ourselves and the world around us.

It will be a battle, but we must fight. Paul recognized the battle: "The weapons we fight with are not the weapons of the world. On the contrary, they have divine power to demolish strongholds. We demolish arguments and every pretension that sets itself up against the knowledge of God, and we take captive every thought to make it obedient to Christ" (2 Corinthians 10:4, 5, NIV).

Are you ready to demolish the strongholds the enemy has built in your life? Are you ready to destroy every negative, critical story he's spoken into your life in an attempt to keep you from being the person God has created you to be, including every lie he's told you about God and what He thinks about you?

Take every thought captive, and make it obedient to Christ.

It's time to stop and really hear what we're thinking—the stories we're telling ourselves—and hold our thoughts up against the truth of God's Word. It's time to stop repeating or believing anything that doesn't line up with what God says about Himself and about us.

I have a simple three-part strategy for doing this in my own life: (1) recognize, (2) reject, and (3) replace.

First, recognize. We need to be aware of and learn to recognize the enemy. He can be subtle. His words may be negative and critical. They may cause us to want to hide or shrink. They may cause us to try and stay busy so that we don't have time to connect with people. And the enemy doesn't just try to keep us busy with unimportant things. He loves to keep us too busy for what God really wants. These can be good things, even church related, but they are not what God has called us to do. The enemy also tries to keep us so busy that we don't have time for relationships or our families. He wants us to feel guilt and shame. Neither is a good motivator for change. They just discourage and become a prison that keeps us from God's promised joy, peace, hope, and abundant life. Sometimes the things we're feeling guilt or shame over are things we've done. We beat ourselves up again and again instead of going to God for forgiveness and allowing Him to redeem. That's His specialty.

How can we recognize the enemy's voice? By what grows in our hearts and minds as a result: discouragement, shame, guilt, and hopelessness and feelings of being unloved, unwanted, and defeated.

Also, as we learn to hold our thoughts up against God's Word, we'll see the disconnect. Would God ever talk to us that way? What has God promised?

Remember what God's Word tells us is the enemy's goal? He wants to steal, kill, destroy, and devour. Are the things we're telling ourselves doing any of these things? Stealing our joy? Destroying our relationships? Killing our peace? Devouring our hope and courage? The Bible tells us that Jesus brings life and brings it abundantly (John 10:10). Are the stories we're telling ourselves bringing us life, courage, and hope? Are they causing us to be more of who God created us to be? If not, we are listening to the enemy instead of God.

Second, reject. If a thought isn't from God, just let it go—every thought, every time. Tell yourself, *No, I'm not going to believe that.* You may need to say aloud, "Not today, Satan."

I remember one women's retreat where the speaker, Celina Dawson, taught us a little hand movement—a twist of the arm, moving your hand up as if to stop someone. Then she got us to say, "I do not receive that." Try it. Go ahead. I'll be right here when you get back. Stand up. Move your arm and hand to create a stop sign of sorts and say, "I do not receive that."

Feels pretty good, doesn't it? It may sound silly, but I can't tell you how often those friends and I who listened to Celina that day have repeated the lesson with each other. You can't do it every time a not-enough thought goes through your head, but do it a few times. Practice. Choose one of God's promises to repeat in your head when the negative, critical words begin to flow and you start losing your focus on God and His enoughness and look at your not enoughness instead. I tell myself, "Don't let the enemy win."

Third, replace. It's not enough to recognize and reject the enemy's words. That leaves an empty spot that needs to be filled. We need to replace negative thinking with God's Word. We need to know who we are. We need to learn and know what God says about us, choose to believe it, memorize it, and highlight it in our Bibles.

My friend Ginny Allen once said that she likes to underline the words God has spoken about her in purple ink in her Bible, so they pop out. I have friends who draw pictures or create word art in the margins of their Bibles as visual reminders of what God is speaking to them. Post verses that speak to you in places that you'll see throughout your day. Use these verses as passwords and screen savers. Scatter other visuals that speak of God's love and belief in you around as reminders. Use things that, at a glance, will remind you of who you are in Christ and who He is to you.

Taking every thought captive, recognizing the enemy, rejecting what he says, and replacing our thoughts with what God says is true will help us to start telling ourselves new stories that, like the woman with the issue of blood, will grow the faith and courage that lead to healing. We just need to get to Jesus.

New stories

Like the woman, we can start talking to ourselves and telling ourselves new stories.

New stories about ourselves. We are pretty good at talking to ourselves in the mirror, in the car, at work, at home, or while out with friends. In fact, we talk to ourselves more than any other person. Let's start telling ourselves better stories about who we are and what we are capable of doing with God.

Look in the mirror, and instead of beating yourself up about your extra weight or wrinkles, tell yourself about what God is doing through you. Remind yourself about what makes you beautiful instead of recounting what you think makes you not beautiful enough:

- You have a caring heart.
- You have the gift of listening to others.
- You have the ability to make amazing chocolate-chip cookies to share with others and brighten their day. (Talking to you, Cheri!)
- You have the endurance to run a half marathon, knowing you won't come in first or near the top ten at all, but you will finish. (Way to go, Pam!)
- You didn't give up on life or your kids when your husband gave up on you. It's been hard, but you're pushing through the loneliness and making memories with your children.
- You lost someone you loved—someone who seemed like your whole world—but you're still getting up each morning and facing the new day, slowly getting stronger and more confident with each step.

- You have the ability to make every single one of your grandkids feel like they're your favorite. (And they're not telling the others!)
- You open your house to kids who need a home.
- No matter how busy you are, you make time when a friend needs a listening ear, a cup of tea, and a scone.
- You have a gift for growing things.
- You have the courage to swallow your fear and talk to the person who is alone in the corner while others are talking and laughing together around the room.

Tell yourself what God says about you: You are "fearfully and wonderfully made" (Psalm 139:14). You are the apple of His eye (see Psalm 17:8). You were created in His image for a purpose (see Genesis 1:27). He has loved you with "an everlasting love" (Jeremiah 31:3). He has a plan for your life (Jeremiah 29:11). He "will never leave you" or abandon you (Hebrews 13:5).

New stories about our sin and bad habits. Instead of talking about being defeated, let's remind ourselves that God has given us victory. When we're tempted to give in to that habitual sin—the thing we don't want to do yet still want to do—we can tell ourselves, "God has given me victory. I don't need to do this any longer. He gives me the strength to stop." The Bible promises that if we "resist the devil," "he will flee" (James 4:7). Let's get some resisting going on.

When we sin, mess up, fail at something, or lean on chocolate when we're stressed instead of on God, we can tell ourselves the truth. We are sinners. We will fail and mess up. But we are not failures. We can confess our sin, knowing that God promises to forgive (1 John 1:9). Instead of beating ourselves up for failing again, thank God that He never gives up on us. Ask Him to continue working on us, redeeming us, and changing us.

New stories about others. Too often when people don't talk to us, we assume it's about us. We're not enough. They don't like us. We did something to offend them. We avoid the people who are mean, critical, or hurtful. We watch the women who seem to have it all together and feel less than. We don't reach out to them. Why would they want to be friends with us?

Let's ask God to show us people through His eyes. Is it possible that lack of response is because they're battling themselves? Is it possible that the woman who has it all together is struggling in areas that no one sees, and she could use a friend? How happy can the negative, critical person really be? Remember that the enemy is out to steal, kill, destroy, and devour every single one of us. We are all battling. Each of us faces challenges that no one else knows about—things we don't talk about—fears, sin, and negative stories that run through our heads. If we knew other people's stories, we might understand why they act as they do. We can ask God to show us how to love and care for other people in tangible ways.

The next time someone doesn't talk to you or seems to insult you in some way, tell yourself it's not about you but about the battles in this person's life. Send up a prayer. Ask for wisdom. Pray for courage, and then connect with him or her. Talk to the person face to face, or send a note, text, or email. Just let this individual know you were thinking about and praying for him or her. Don't do this to get a response that you can see, but do it so that God can work in this person's life. The next time someone is mean and critical, ask God for a way to encourage him or her. Speak positively in reply to this person, instead of slapping back with words or avoiding him or her.

New stories from our past. Are there stories from your past that still hurt? You can ask God to reframe and redeem them. Invite Him to speak into the stories and bring new perspectives and understanding. Ask for the courage to forgive those who hurt you, whether the wound was intentional or not. Give Him the story to use to impact others.

There is a story from my past that wounded me. It made me feel I wasn't pretty enough and wasn't wanted. And it was a story my mom seemed to love to tell people. I hated when she told it. I've heard it so many times I actually have a visual "video" of it playing in my head as I tell it. (And these days she no longer tells it, but I do. God has redeemed it—I'll get to that part—and made it a funny story to me now.) It's from my birth. Mom was only seven months pregnant when she went into labor with me. It was a crazy weekend at the hospital. There were lots of babies, so many that there weren't enough labor-and-delivery rooms. (This was back when there were labor-and-delivery rooms, and women were put to sleep and woke up later with a baby.) I was her first baby, and I was early, so Mom was nervous. They wheeled her away, and the next thing she remembers is waking up in a hospital room. She knew her baby had been born, but no one told her whether it was a girl or boy, how big, or even whether the baby was OK. Her roommate received her baby—her fourth or fifth one. He was a big, healthy baby. Nurses brought him in throughout the morning and early afternoon for his mom to feed. But no baby was brought to my mom. Distraught, she didn't eat breakfast or lunch. Finally, her doctor showed up and wanted to know why she wasn't eating. When he learned that she hadn't seen her baby yet, he sent a nurse out for me. I was small but healthy.

This is where the story gets a little crazy and was hard for my little-girl heart that heard it repeated. Mom recalls the nurse bringing her baby wrapped in a blue blanket, despite the doctor saying I was a girl. When she opened the blanket, she saw a small, dark, and hairy baby. Supposedly the hair covering my body was so long that you could braid it down my back. (My mom does love to tell a story and make it a bit more dramatic sometimes.) Then she always said, "I couldn't believe this was my baby! It looked like a monkey!"

What was supposed to be a humorous story wasn't funny to my little-girl heart. The enemy translated those words as, "You are not pretty. You are so unattractive that even your own mom didn't want you." Now please know that my mom didn't mean any harm. She loves me. For her, it was an innocent, fun story to tell. She wasn't the problem. The enemy was. He loves to twist things and use them to steal, kill, and destroy.

As I realized the damage caused by the story, I began praying and asking God to redeem and use it. I recognize that He's used this story and others to make me an empathetic person who longs to encourage people and help them know that they are loved. It's one of the main messages I seek to share with others: God loves them. He believes they are beautiful. He wants them. He has a purpose and a plan for their lives. This story and others like it shaped how I saw myself, but all that changed when I discovered a God who loves me. His love and what He says brought—and continues to bring—courage, hope, and healing. I want others to experience that too.

One day I was alone, rummaging through a box of my granny's old pictures. Mom told me that I could go through them and have any that I wanted. They were random photos all thrown together in a box from various years and people. Gran never put her photos in albums or organized them in any way. Most of the time, she didn't even write names on the back or anything to identify the picture. There were photos of relatives. Some I recognized; some I didn't. There were photos of babies, children, my granny's sisters and their families picnicking on the ground, or family members sitting in my great-granny's house with the remainders of dinner on the table. As I pulled one baby picture from the box, something about it caught my heart. I'm not one of those people who gush over newborn babies. But this one was different. Obviously a hospital photo, the baby was tiny and beautiful. The photo brought me joy. Then I flipped it over. (You're getting ahead of me, aren't you?) Gran had written on this one: "Tamyra Lynn DeVoe, May 26." This was a picture of me! That beautiful newborn baby, who didn't look anything like a monkey, was me! God had brought healing, and then He brought the picture.

New stories about God. Remember that the enemy isn't out to destroy just us but also how we see God. He wants us to believe that God doesn't really love us. Everyone else, yes, but not us. He wants us to believe that God loves us but is typically pretty frustrated with us. If he can, he'd like us to believe that God is a stern judge, just waiting for us to fail. He will tempt us to believe that God is hard to please or that He's given up on us. None of these stories are true. They don't match up with what the Bible tells us. We need to make sure we're telling ourselves true stories about God.

God loves us—always has and always will. We can't make Him love us more, and we can't make Him love us less. He loved us, knowing completely who we are and how we would fail. He knows better than we do the areas where we are not enough, where we battle, where we are defeated, where we wrestle, and where we give up. Yet He chose us.

God knows we are sinners. That's why He sent Jesus to die for us and why He offers us forgiveness when we ask. He will convict but never guilt and shame us into discouragement. He will convict us into repentance and restoration.

God is for us, believes in us, and is cheering us on. He's sent His angels to protect us and His Holy Spirit to guide and counsel us. "Every spiritual blessing" in Christ is ours (Ephesians 1:3). With God for us, no one and nothing can stand in our way (see Romans 8:31). He will never give up on us (Deuteronomy 31:6, Matthew 28:20).

God created us in His image (Genesis 1:27). He wrote our stories in His Book (Psalm 139). He knows us—all about us, every inch, every hair, every freckle, and every scar—and He loves us. He wants more for us than we can want for ourselves. His plans are bigger than ours. We can trust Him.

What are you telling yourself about God, especially in those moments when you've failed, sinned, or given up on yourself? Tell yourself a new story. Get into God's Word, and memorize what He says is true about Himself and about you. Claim those promises. Believe Him, not the enemy.

Gratitude journal

As we begin to tell ourselves new stories, rejecting the stories the enemy wants us to believe, gratitude can be a powerful component to rewiring our thinking. Recording the things for which we are grateful helps us to tell ourselves a new story. Instead of remembering and recounting all the negatives, disappointments, and failures, we focus on the positives, successes, and gifts.

One way to do this is by simply keeping a gratitude journal. It can be handwritten or kept in a file on your mobile device or computer. Every day write down things or moments for which you are grateful. Numerous articles and blogs recommend listing three to five items each day. I've challenged myself and others to list ten. Try to come up with new things every day. When I'm trying to list ten new items each day, it causes me to go through my day, intentionally looking for things. Yesterday I was grateful for the following:

1. Blue skies and gorgeous fall weather.
2. An unexpected compliment from my brother-in-law. (God knew I was disappointed that I never found a great new dress for an event and had pulled something from my closet, which I hadn't worn in years.)
3. The way my youngest son gently and lovingly encouraged his wife and gave her a hug when she was stressed.
4. Kaleigh's joy and laughter.
5. A yummy chocolate-chip cookie.
6. My oldest son's smile.
7. His wife's joy and their friendship.
8. Texts from friends saying they were praying for the day ahead.
9. My husband being silly.
10. Getting to know my youngest son's in-laws a bit more.

Just writing the list made me smile and remember good moments from the day. Practicing gratitude changes your perspective when you think back through your day and look for the good things. I tend to make a list early in the morning when I'm hanging out with God. I remember the day before and the ways God spoke into these moments.

A harder challenge would be to list things you are grateful to God for about the way He created you. We can all list the things we'd love to change, but what are we grateful for about ourselves? I've always been thankful that I am flexible and don't mind change, even at the last minute. I'm grateful to be empathetic and that I care about others. I'm thankful that I enjoy learning and am typically willing and even desire to learn new things. Now it's your turn. What are three things you are grateful for about who God created you to be? Go ahead. It's OK. This isn't pride or self-promotion. This is gratitude for a God who intentionally designed you to be you because He wanted *you*.

It's also important to think about the things that you're grateful for about God. I'm thankful for His patience, His love, that He never gives up on us, and that He relentlessly pursues us. Sometimes when I need to switch up my thinking from defeated to victorious, I specifically and intentionally take the time to begin thanking God for who He is and all He's done in my life.

One of my favorite stories of gratitude is told by Katie Davis Majors in her book *Daring to Hope*. Katie is a young woman who moved to Uganda and began a ministry that helps children access education and food and empowers moms to work and support their families. Katie also adopted thirteen orphan girls, even though it meant being a single mom for a time. During one particularly tough season in her life, Katie struggled. She was tired—not of serving but of the grief and hard things she saw around her. She didn't feel like she was enough to meet all the needs, and while she knew God was enough, hard things still happened in people's lives every day in her community. Katie turned to gratitude. She began writing things for which she was grateful on Post-it Notes and putting them on the wall of her kitchen. The list grew over days and weeks, covering her walls. It became an instant visual of all God had done and was doing and who He was. It gave her the courage to dare to hope and trust even when life didn't turn out the way she wanted.[1]

Remember

Gratitude is a way of remembering. It's something God often told His people to do: Remember. Remember how He has led. Remember who He is. Remember His commitment to you. Remember your commitment to Him. Keep reminding yourself and telling yourself these stories so that it resets the thinking in your head and heart. It becomes the truth you believe about Him and about yourself.

One of my favorite stories is found in 2 Chronicles 20. King Jehoshaphat and his people are surrounded by an enemy out to destroy them. The enemy is larger than they are. They don't know what to do. Even Jehoshaphat is afraid. He calls the people together and prays. His prayer is filled with remembrances.

- *He remembers who God is.* "LORD, the God of our ancestors, are you not the God who is in heaven? You rule over all the kingdoms of the nations. Power and might are in your hand, and no one can withstand you" (verse 6, NIV).
- *He remembers what God has done.* "Our God, did you not drive out the inhabitants of this land before your people Israel and give it forever to the descendants of Abraham your friend?" (verse 7, NIV).
- *He remembers their commitment.* " 'If calamity comes upon us, whether the sword of judgment, or plague or famine, we will stand in your presence before this temple that bears your Name and will cry out to you in our distress, and you will hear us and save us.' . . . For we have no power to face this vast army that is attacking us. We do not know what to do, but our eyes are on you" (verses 9, 12, NIV).

The people march out the next day, singing praises and thanks to God. While they're on their way, God defeats the enemy. They spend the next three days gathering treasures from a battle they didn't fight.

Remembering refocuses and rebuilds our courage. God knew that we needed to remember. He knew that when life got hard and the enemy got loud, we'd forget. So He challenged us to remember. His people often retold the stories to their children of how He had led them, protected them, provided for them, and guided them. The generations recounted the stories over and over. In the retelling, there is remembrance—feeling the emotions again, being grateful, and bringing courage and hope that He can do it again.

Take a moment to remember. How has God led you? What has He spoken into your life? How has He revealed His love for you?

I remember sitting in the lodge at a camp. Pastor John Kent, the speaker for the event, had challenged us to find a quiet place to sit, pray, and invite God to speak into our hearts. As I sat there in the quiet with God, I could picture myself sitting with Jesus under a tree. Then crazily, I pictured Him laughing, not at me but over me with great joy and delight. I felt like God whispered to me, *"You are My daughter. I delight in you."* I was overwhelmed with emotion. Who had ever delighted in me? The God of the universe said He delighted in me?

Back home, the enemy attempted to steal my joy and hope from that moment. He tempted me to believe that I just let my imagination run wild, I made it up, it wasn't God, and He didn't delight in me.

A couple of months later, I was at the same event, but it was being held at a different location. John was again leading. This time I spent much of the weekend cooking in the kitchen. Discouraged and exhausted, I sat in the room for the final presentation. John encouraged people to gather in groups of three and pray for one another, inviting God to give them a word of encouragement for the others in the group. The silence in our group was broken by a woman I didn't know well. She, too, knew me but not well. She definitely didn't know about my experience from the previous event. Yet she began talking hesitantly to me: "Tami, I know this is going to sound strange, but I think God wants you to know that you're His daughter, and I just picture Him laughing—not at you but with you."

Tears flowed. She couldn't have known, but God did. In His great love, He wanted me to know the true story of who I am. I am His daughter, in whom He takes great delight. I told John the two stories after the event. He said, "Tami, God wants to make sure you don't forget that He delights in you."

Remember: tell yourself a new story—God's story.

Your story

- What are the stories you've told yourself over and over about who you are? About who God is and what He thinks of you? About what others think of you?
- How easy is it for you to recognize the enemy's voice and temptations? What's your game plan for recognizing and rejecting his stories about you and about God?
- How will you replace the enemy's story with God's story? What is one thing you will do to start telling yourself God's story about you? About Him?
- Decide how you will keep a gratitude journal—handwritten, on your computer or mobile device, or Post-it Notes on the wall—and begin challenging yourself to be grateful.
- How has God led you? What has He done in your life? What are the stories you remember about how God has revealed Himself and His love for you? Retell the stories to yourself and to someone else. There's something about telling another person the story.

God is enough

God is enough to redeem the stories you've believed, and He will help you to believe a new story about Him and about yourself.

Promise

"For the weapons of our warfare are not carnal but mighty in God for pulling down strongholds, casting down arguments and every high thing that exalts itself against the knowledge of God, bringing every thought into captivity to the obedience of Christ" (2 Corinthians 10:4, 5).

Prayer

Father God, You are mighty. You have led us, protected us, and provided for us in ways we don't even realize. You've chosen us to be Your daughters, who are loved and wanted. Our story is a love story set in a battle. It ends with the only true happily ever after—eternity with You in a place that You've planned and created just for us. Until that day, Lord, please open our eyes to see the enemy's attacks. Give us the courage and desire to reject his stories, resist his temptations, and tell ourselves the truth. You are God, and we are Yours. You want us. You forgive us. You enable us to resist temptation. You give us the courage to share about You with others. Help us to replace the messages that we are not enough from our past with the belief that You are enough for today and tomorrow. Speak into those past memories and wounds. Show them to us from Your perspective. Use them to change our world for You. Father, we love You. We want more of You. We want to walk confidently as Your daughters. In Jesus' name, amen.

---

1. For more of Katie's inspiring story, read Katie Davis Majors, *Kisses From Katie* (New York: Howard Books, 2011) and *Daring to Hope* (New York: Multnomah, 2017).

Chapter 14

When We've Blown It

S ometimes we fail. We give in to the temptation to do something, think something, or act in a way we shouldn't. We rely on ourselves instead of God, and it doesn't go well. We fall into the same sin again and again. We say we're going to quit, and we do for a time. Then, in a moment of weakness, there we go again. We indulge in

- pride,
- selfishness,
- a critical, judging spirit,
- a little lie,
- a bad habit,
- a flirtation that makes us feel pretty and seen, or
- a bitter, unforgiving spirit because some person doesn't deserve forgiveness.

While we want to stop, we really don't want to either. But this sin is hurting us.

Sometimes we feel like we're not enough because, in truth, we're not enough. What do we do when we've blown it?

Sadly, these are the moments the enemy loves. He likes to tempt us to believe that God is unhappy with us. The enemy wants us to believe that God won't forgive us again; maybe the first few times, but by now, we should have our act together. The enemy wants to use the ways we've blown it or failed and cover us with a shame that keeps us from living the lives God longs for us to live.

"There are moments in our lives when we fail so badly that we feel absolutely unworthy to receive the grace of God. And it is those moments of vulnerability that make us or break us spiritually. Either we lock ourselves in the cage of guilt and never come out, or we discover new dimensions of God's grace."[1]

Pride goes before a fall

Peter was about to fail so badly that he would wrestle with guilt, shame, and bitterness. But he would also have the opportunity to choose whether to stay in that emotional prison or be set free by God's grace.

Jesus tried to warn him, but Peter thought he knew himself better. "Simon,

Simon! Indeed, Satan has asked for you, that he may sift you as wheat. But I have prayed for you, that your faith should not fail; and when you have returned to Me, strengthen your brethren" (Luke 22:31, 32).

I don't know about you, but I find part of what Jesus is saying to be a bit scary. The enemy had asked to sift Peter—to try him and see what he is made of. It sounds very much like Job's story. Is it our story too? The enemy is tempting us, sifting us, to see how real and strong our commitment to God is. Do we really trust Him? Will we cling to Him no matter what happens? I'm afraid the enemy knows us so well that the test can come in the hardest and most precious areas for our hearts.

Other parts of what Jesus tells Peter bring me courage: "But I have prayed for you, that your faith should not fail; and when you have returned to Me, strengthen your brethren" (verse 32).

Jesus is praying for Peter and for us. Even now, as He sits by His Father in heaven, He is interceding for us. And He's been here. He knows the battles, the temptations, and how hard life can be. He gets it. So He prays for us like someone who has been here and knows—because He does.

He prays that Peter's faith won't fail. Does He pray for Peter's faith in himself? No. Before the night is over, Peter will beat himself up like he never has before. Jesus is praying for Peter's faith in Him and his trust in God's love. Peter's been walking with Jesus for three years. He's seen the miracles, heard the teachings, and experienced more than anyone else; he's part of Jesus' inner circle of friends. He's walked on water. He's performed miracles himself when Jesus sent the disciples out. He's experienced Jesus' patience, kindness, and caring. Jesus healed his mother-in-law and provided his business with a boatload of fish. Jesus wants Peter to remember those moments and how He always came through and loved him.

"When you have returned to Me." Did you catch what Jesus is implying here? In order to return, Peter has to leave. He's going to fall and walk away. But he will also wrestle it through and eventually return to following Jesus. Jesus is so sure of these events that He gives Peter a task to do afterward: Strengthen your brothers. Give them courage. Share your experience, and help them to remember that God forgives and redeems.

But Peter is too full of self and pride. "Lord, I am ready to go with You, both to prison and to death" (verse 33). No doubt, he is sincere. He wants to be this committed to Jesus, but he is relying on himself and his pride, and he's weaker than he realizes. The other disciples add their agreement; they, too, are ready to go to prison or die with Jesus.

Jesus warns him, "I tell you, Peter, the rooster shall not crow this day before you will deny three times that you know Me" (verse 34).

Too late

After a few more words, Jesus and His disciples head out to the Garden. The first battle with the enemy took place in a garden. Now another eternity-impacting battle will also happen in a garden. How does Jesus spend these last moments with His disciples before the Cross? What are His last words of advice?

Prayer.

Three times Jesus tells the disciples to pray in order to prepare themselves for the coming temptation. He knows what they are about to face and how it will shake their faith and thinking. He knows about the doubts, the fears, and the questioning. He knows about Peter's fall and the resulting shame and guilt. He didn't tell them that if they prayed, they wouldn't be tempted. He tells them to pray so that they can stand up to the temptation.

Jesus Himself prays. As He heads into the Garden, the weight and darkness of sin descend on Him. He feels alone. The enemy fights intensely, knowing that in this garden the battle will be won or lost. This is his last chance to destroy and thwart God's plan. We can't comprehend the full battle. Jesus, who has walked with the Father forever and has felt His presence and approval even here on Earth, no longer senses God. Instead, He is filled with the heaviness of sin and separation. God feels distant and silent. While God may feel silent, the enemy is loud and relentless. He has been preparing for this moment. He has watched Jesus for the last three years and planned his attack. The enemy desires to push Jesus to say no and give up on us. Now, when Jesus needs the prayers of His friends, He finds them sleeping. His closest friends can't keep their eyes open when He needs them most. Mark records in his account of the story that Jesus specifically calls Peter out, challenging him to pray for even just an hour so that he doesn't give in to temptation.

"And while He was still speaking . . ." (Luke 22:47). According to Mark 14, He wakes them a third time, but it is too late. The multitude has come for Jesus. There is no time to pray and no time to prepare. The enemy is here in human form.

A sword, an ear, and the gospel

"When those around Him saw what was going to happen, they said to Him, 'Lord, shall we strike with the sword?' " (Luke 22:49).

They had counted their swords before they left the upper room. There were two. Now they're ready to prove their words: they will go to prison or die with Jesus. Peter doesn't wait for an answer. He grabs a sword and takes a swing. But he's a fisherman, not a soldier. His attempt cuts off the ear of the servant of the high priest. Was Peter attempting to prove himself to Jesus—show that he wouldn't fall and was willing to go to prison or die—and prove his worthiness and commitment?

I can relate to Peter. I sometimes want to fight and keep the hard stuff away, misunderstanding how necessary it may be and what it will accomplish. I much prefer life to be easy and comfortable.

But Jesus simply puts the ear back on the shocked guy. Jesus is willing to be accused and crucified because He knows what it will accomplish. This is what He has come to do—die for our sins and provide the sacrifice so we can live eternally.

Did you notice whose ear Peter cut off? The servant of the high priest. Of all the people there, he manages to hit that one. The high priest is not a fan of Jesus or His disciples. This band of soldiers and leaders are there because the high priest and religious leaders want to stop Jesus. If they have a chance to take out His disciples, especially one of the most outspoken, they will. And here could be an opportunity.

Imagine for a moment: The multitude gets back to town, and the servant tells the high priest what has happened. Everyone corroborates the story, pointing to Peter as the culprit. The high priest presses charges. Peter is taken to court for attempted murder and assault with a deadly weapon. Being sent to prison or death—that could really happen now.

In court, the prosecution calls witness after witness. They all say the same thing. They all point to Peter. It's not looking good. The prosecution even calls the other disciples. They have to tell the truth. They saw Peter do it. If the prosecution could call Peter to the stand, he'd have to admit to it too. He did it. Everyone saw it.

Then it's the defense's turn. The defense calls just one witness—the servant. He asks just one question: "Which ear did my client allegedly cut off?"

The servant points to his ear. But remember, Jesus has put the ear back on. And when Jesus heals, He heals well. It's not crooked. There is no scar. In fact, it probably looks better than the other one. There is no evidence that it's ever been cut off.

The judge has no choice. He throws out the case.

Friends, that's our story. When we sin and ask Jesus to forgive us of our sins, He not only forgives but also removes our sin "as far as the east is from the west" (Psalm 103:12). He cleanses us "from all unrighteousness" (1 John 1:9). When God looks at us, He sees us through the sacrifice and blood of Jesus: "Through the righteousness of Christ we shall stand before God pardoned, and as though we had never sinned."[2] *As though we had never sinned.*" Jesus redeems our lives as neatly as He healed the servant's ear.

Distance

Despite the fact that Jesus heals the man's ear, they arrest Him. They're not interested in the truth. They just don't want Him messing up their lives or the way they've always done things. They lead him to the home of the high priest, where He will be accused, abused, questioned, and ultimately sent to the cross.

"But Peter followed at a distance" (Luke 22:54).

Peter doesn't understand what just happened. He tried to rescue Jesus, but Jesus didn't want to be rescued. Jesus being arrested and led away in chains isn't what Peter expects. He thought Jesus was going to rescue them from Roman rule and set up a kingdom here on Earth. Peter was going to serve in the new kingdom. This just doesn't make sense, so he follows at a distance. He wants to see how the story plays out but doesn't want to stand out. Fear, doubt, questions, and disappointment—they begin to fill his thoughts.

"Peter sat among them" (verse 55).

He finds a seat near the fire. It's the cool of the night. He can blend into the crowd here yet still see what's happening across the courtyard with Jesus. Note the fire. There are two stories in the Gospels that include a fire. This is the first one. The second is coming.

As Peter sits there, someone starts staring at him curiously. He tries to avoid looking at her. He doesn't want her to make the connection.

"This man was also with Him."
But he denied Him, saying, "Woman, I do not know Him' " (verses 56, 57).

Maybe he told himself that he didn't know *this* Jesus. He knew the Jesus who overturned tables and called the Pharisees whitewashed tombs. But not this Jesus who submitted to arrest and abuse. This was not the Messiah he was expecting. The enemy was attempting to convince him that it was a lie. Jesus wasn't who He said He was and who Peter thought He was. Peter didn't really know Him after all.

Two more times people speak up and identify Peter as one of the disciples. Both times Peter denies it. He's afraid. He no longer wants prison or death. He just wants to fade into the darkness of the night. But the night sky is fading, and the dawn is rising. And roosters begin to crow.

"Immediately, while he was still speaking, the rooster crowed. And the Lord turned and looked at Peter" (verses 60, 61).

While he's denying knowing Jesus, he hears the rooster crow. Jesus' words replay in his mind. Without even thinking about it, Peter turns to look at Jesus across the courtyard. Their eyes meet. In these few seconds of connection, Jesus needs to "speak" into Peter's heart without using words. He can't call out, but He can look.

Your mom may have had a look. Just one look and you knew you were about to get in trouble. Or her look could make you think twice and stop what you were doing. But this isn't that look. Jesus doesn't want to scold or accuse or guilt Peter. He wants to convey love. He wants Peter to remember the rest of what He said: He was praying for him, praying for faith. He wanted Peter to remember His love and His forgiveness and to trust Him even in this moment of betrayal.

Conviction, guilt, and shame flood over him, not just for denying Jesus but for doubting, mistrusting, and not having faith. He recognizes that he has let Jesus down on so many levels. He is convicted of his sin, his bold statement, and fearful failure. He leaves brokenhearted and repentant, weeping bitterly. He will never forget this moment.

Giving up

The enemy doesn't want Peter to forget. Each morning as a new day rises and roosters begin to crow around the villages, the enemy will remind Peter of his failure. The enemy does the same to us. It may not be roosters crowing, but he will find ways to persistently remind us of our failures. He won't let them go, especially if we haven't forgiven ourselves. Our lack of forgiveness provides him with opportunities to keep dredging them up and beating us up with what we've done wrong.

Peter is no longer bold and confident. He is broken. He no longer believes he is good enough to be a disciple. How can he preach about Jesus when he failed Him so miserably and after everything he said? He goes back to what he does know: fishing.

"Simon Peter said to them, 'I am going fishing' " (John 21:3).

If he can't be a disciple, he can be a fisherman. He'd made a living at it before. He can do it again. Other disciples go with him. They're all feeling a little lost. Peter has been a leader, but he's not leading anymore. Yet they still follow, unsure what else to do. Their world has been turned upside down. Maybe a night on the water will be good for them.

Have you ever given up on yourself? Felt like you had failed one too many times? Thought you were never going to get it right? Believed someone like you had nothing to offer God? Can you relate to Peter's story? I hope so. Because it's about to go from bad to worse to amazing. Our story becomes amazing too. Hang in there. Don't give up.

They fish all night and catch nothing. *Nothing.* Not one little fish. Imagine the disciples on this lake where they had experienced so much of Christ. During this night of not catching anything and just sitting, their minds wander and remember. Peter remembers times from the last three years: the feeding of the five thousand, Jesus' healings and teachings, the night He calmed the storm with just a word, walking on water and sinking as his eyes and faith slipped. Now he had sunk even lower, remembering Jesus' face across the courtyard. Could he ever forgive himself? Could Jesus?

Slowly, the sky begins to lighten. Glimpses of color streak the horizon as the night fades into a new day. And then the roosters' crowing begins from all the villages around the lake. The sound echoes across the water and fills the boat, waking Peter from his memories. He realizes that night is over, and he hasn't caught anything. He's a failure as a disciple and a failure as a fisherman. He can't do anything right. The crowing echoes in his ears.

But the story isn't over

As the disciples row toward the shore, a voice calls out to them. A Man is standing on the beach. "Have you caught anything?"

Fishermen like that question when their nets are full but not as much when they haven't caught anything. The disciples tell him no. I'm not sure why they did it. They don't know who is calling out to them in the early gray of dawn. Does He know anything about fishing? It doesn't matter. He tells them to cast their nets, and they do. Suddenly, they can't pull their nets in because of the number of fish. (Someone impressed by the catch later counts it: 153 large fish.)

John suddenly realizes this has happened before! When Christ called Peter, Andrew, James, and John three years earlier, they had just finished fishing all night and caught nothing. Jesus told them to cast their nets, and they did. The catch was so great that it took two boats to bring it to shore. That's when He had called them to follow Him and be fishers of men.

"It's Jesus!" John shouts.

Peter is excited. *Jesus!* He puts on his clothes, jumps in the water, rushes to the beach, and then stops dead in his tracks. There's Jesus standing by a fire. A fire. The last time their eyes met over a fire, he had denied even knowing Him—the greatest regret and failure of his life.

There is something different about this fire. Jesus is using it to cook a breakfast of fish and bread. It sounds like something from another miracle: fish, bread, and feeding five thousand. They had doubted Jesus and not wanted to bother, but He had taken the little they had and filled the bellies of more than five thousand people. There were more leftovers than what they had started with! It's astonishing what God can do with just a little bit. Can He do something with Peter's little bit of faith?

It's pretty amazing to me that the risen Savior provides bread and fish and comes and builds a fire. It's down to the coals, so He's been waiting there for a while. Then He cooks breakfast for these messy, doubting men. God's love is awesome, isn't it? He did all of that for guys who had doubted and hidden themselves away, who failed Him and denied Him, and who couldn't even pray with Him when He needed them. He keeps pursuing, loving, wooing, and inviting.

He does this for you too. He loves you just like He did the disciples. He will move heaven and earth for you, leaving the ninety-nine to go in search of you. This God is more than enough, even when you're a mess and even when you've given up on yourself.

I still choose you

After breakfast, Jesus asks Peter three times, "Do you love Me?" (verses 15–17). Peter responds, "Yes, Lord; You know that I love You" (verse 15). Much has been written about this conversation. Scholars look at the words that Jesus and Peter each use for "love." Today I just want you to see one thing: Jesus redeeming every moment of Peter's life.

He redeems the three denials with His three invitations for Peter to affirm his love.

He redeems the fire. Now when Peter looks at a fire, he will remember the first time and the denial, but he will also remember the second time and Jesus cooking him breakfast, freely offering forgiveness and acceptance.

He redeems the early morning. When the rooster crows, the enemy will remind Peter of his failure, but the Holy Spirit will remind him of this moment, of Jesus waiting on the shore, of redemption and forgiveness.

He re-creates the original call on Peter's life. It's as though Jesus is saying, "I called you then, I call you now. I know everything that's happened in between, and I still choose you. Follow Me."

Follow Me.

Peter can choose to believe Jesus and accept His forgiveness and grace. He can choose to live this moment of redemption and restoration and be the fisher of men that God created him to be. Or he can choose to stay locked in his shame and guilt. He can live chained to his failure and his past. He can believe that he is nothing more than a rough, uneducated fisherman who too often speaks and acts without thinking. He can believe that God has given up on him, just like he has given up on himself. He can believe that there's no way God can use him.

It's a choice we each get to choose: live in the belief that we are forgiven, chosen, and wanted, or live believing we'll never get it right or be enough for God to use. Peter chose to accept Christ's invitation. The Bible tells us that he and the other disciples turned the world upside down. They shared the gospel, and lives were changed for eternity. Others saw the difference. "When they [Jerusalem's rulers and elders] saw the courage of Peter and John and realized that they were unschooled, ordinary men, they were astonished and they took note that these men had been with Jesus" (Acts 4:13, NIV).

Your choice

I'll never forget one woman's story. I wish I knew more about where it went from the last chapter I witnessed. I pray for her when she comes to mind—pray that she eventually chose Jesus.

She was born to a mom who loved her and a dad who abused her verbally and physically. She heard the message from her father painfully loud and clear. She was never good enough; no matter how hard she tried or what she did. She was smart and athletic—Olympic-team level athletic—until an injury sidelined her. Her mom eventually left her father and married a man who also loved her. Her mom and stepdad encouraged her and cheered her on. But her dad's words rang loudly in her head.

He wasn't the only man who verbally and physically assaulted her. When she started dating, it's not surprising that she chose a man much like her father. It's what she knew and was comfortable with. Like most abusive men, he distanced her from her family and friends and controlled her life and her communications. I'm not sure what gave her the courage to leave, but at some point, she'd had enough and called her mom.

That's when I met her. She had moved back home with her mom and stepdad. They were helping her get her life back together. She had enrolled in college and planned to finish her degree. I remember when a coaching job opened at a local high school, and she excitedly interviewed and then texted me to say she got the job. I congratulated her and told her I'd been praying for her. She got a car and insurance and met a new guy. He was handsome. And unlike the previous boyfriend, he didn't hit her—with his hand or with his words. He was kind, caring, and considerate. Her parents immediately began talking about marriage. This was the type of man they wanted for their daughter.

Her social media posts reflected that young, new-in-love love: "He makes me feel loved like no one ever has before." He took her out. He held doors open for her. He enjoyed hanging out with her friends and family. Life was good.

One day she disappeared. No one had heard from her by the next day nor could they contact her. She didn't return phone calls or texts. She had told her new boyfriend that a friend had been in an accident and was in the hospital a few hours away. She was going to go visit her. That was the last he heard from her. The next day her mom grew worried and called the friend who had been in an accident, only to discover there hadn't been an accident. She was fine and hadn't talked to this young woman for a couple of weeks.

Mom knew where to call next—the old boyfriend. Her daughter had gone back. The old boyfriend had immediately taken her phone and car keys, eventually took down her social media profiles, attempting to cut her off again from friends and family. As loved ones begged her to come back, his voice raged in the background. "I told you, you'd be back. You're not worth anything else. This is what you deserve."

She believed him. She didn't think she was good enough to be loved by someone who was kind and caring.

You and I may not have a person beating us up. (If you do, leave and get yourself to a safe place.[3]) But we do have an enemy who assaults us with thoughts that tempt us to believe we're not good enough and we're unworthy of God's love or forgiveness. This enemy wants us to believe that God can't possibly be that patient or that, even though God forgives, we're still not enough to serve Him or do anything for Him.

He is lying. We do not need to stay locked in a prison of guilt and shame. We just need to confess our sin, ask for God's forgiveness, and then choose to believe that we are forgiven and that He has a purpose for our lives. God longs to turn the world around us upside down through our gifts and stories.

Sacred pain

Sometimes the not-enough moments, especially our sin and failures, are moments that God uses to call us deeper and refine us in the refiner's fire. These moments burn off the rough edges and things in our hearts and characters that get in the way of what God wants to do in us and through us. It can be painful, but it is a sacred pain—like Peter's experience. Days of reflecting, repenting, and allowing God to speak into the pain make us stronger, more dependent on Him, and more aware of His grace.

I do not like pain or hard things. But sometimes, they are necessary.

I didn't even realize that I had become negative, complaining more than I recognized. I was trying hard, working a ton of hours while juggling multiple projects. I thought my hard work and commitment would bring affirmation and value and open up new opportunities. I was unprepared to learn that my negative, complaining attitude spoke more loudly than my hard work and completed projects. After walking out of a meeting where I discovered what people were thinking and reading into my behavior, I was struggling. No longer sure that my job was secure, I was devastated. I walked around numb and broken for the next two weeks. The pain was so great I just wanted to stay in bed under the covers and not face the new day. But that wasn't an option. There was a conference to attend, meetings to prepare for, and projects to complete. It was a busy time of year for my department. I needed to push through, one foot in front of another. Many days I felt like I was just going through the motions. I tried to smile and engage but was devastated inside. I felt shame, embarrassment, and anger with myself. I was unsure of what to do if I lost my job.

I prayed—a lot. I confessed my negative, critical attitude to my coworkers and apologized. I asked for forgiveness. I had to wrestle with the stories I was telling myself. It was not the end of the world. God had not given up on me. He still loved me and still called me to serve. My coworkers hadn't given up on me either. It was going to be OK. God just needed to get my attention and change me.

It was humbling, embarrassing—and needed. It was one of the most painful moments of my work experience but a sacred pain because of the refining work God was doing in my life.

Sacred pain brings the opportunity to walk through moments meant to refine us and make us more of who God created us to be. It convicts us, sends us to our knees, brings us to repentance, and causes us to surrender more completely. It is also an opportunity to experience God's grace in new ways and encounter His love even in our failure and sin. The enemy will attempt to use sacred pain to destroy us. He'll tempt us to believe stories that aren't true. He will do everything he can to get us to beat ourselves up and not forgive ourselves.

Forgive yourself

I don't know what this woman did, but whatever it was, she couldn't get past it and forgive herself. I attempted to encourage her, "God forgives you. If you confess your sin to Him, He will forgive you."

"I know God forgives me. I just can't forgive myself."

It was one of those moments where I found myself talking without thinking first. "So you're bigger than God?"

She looked at me in surprise. "What do you mean?"

I have to admit that I was a little surprised. I was not quite sure where I was going with this thought. "God forgives you, but you can't. You must know more than He does."

She sat back and thought about it. If God forgave her, why didn't she accept His forgiveness and forgive herself? It was her Peter moment: she could choose to believe God or choose to live chained to guilt and shame. She chose God.

What about you? When you find yourself struggling because you've failed, messed up, fallen into temptation again, are battling with the same sin or a new one, or the enemy tempts you to believe that you're not enough or aren't worthy of following Jesus, what are you going to choose?

Walk into His grace? Stay locked in shame?

I pray that you allow God to redeem every failure and forgive every sin, and you choose to follow Him deeper.

Your story

- Have you ever given up on yourself or felt unworthy to be loved? How can you tell yourself a new story?
- In what areas do you struggle with temptation? Confess them to God. Ask Him to convict you and give you courage. When temptation comes, remind yourself that Jesus died for your victory, and you do not need to give in any longer.
- Have you walked through sacred pain—times when you failed or sinned, and it was incredibly painful? Did you (or can you) let God walk you through the pain and refine you?
- Are there things in your life for which you can't forgive yourself? After reading this chapter, what are you going to choose to do?
- What will be helpful in choosing God next time you've blown it instead of allowing the enemy to beat you up?

God is enough

God is enough even when you've blown it, failed, or sinned.

Promise

"If we confess our sins, he is faithful and just and will forgive us our sins and purify us from all unrighteousness" (1 John 1:9, NIV).

Prayer

Lord and Savior, You are the One who paid the price for our sin, died to set us free, and invite us to come, confess, and receive forgiveness—and not just forgiveness but cleansing from all unrighteousness. We give You the authority to search our hearts and convict us. Show us the places in our lives that You long to redeem. Show us the sins we need to confess. We give You our cherished sins—the ones we don't want to do but can't stop doing. Give us the power to stop. We turn our sins over to You today. Make the sins incredibly distasteful and unpleasant so that we no longer get any satisfaction from them. Give us the courage to claim Your victory and say no. Father, show us the places where we're not forgiving ourselves. Help us to let them go and let Your grace replace the shame and guilt. Refine us, even when it hurts. Help us to trust You and choose You. In Jesus' name, amen.

1. Mark Batterson, *Wild Goose Chase* (Colorado Springs, CO: Multnomah Books, 2008), 107.

2. Ellen G. White, *Our High Calling* (Washington, DC: Review and Herald®, 1961), 48.

3. If you need help, call the National Domestic Violence Hotline (1-800-799-SAFE [7233], or 1-800-787-3224 [TTY]), or the National Sexual Assault Hotline (800-656-HOPE).

Chapter 15

Peace That Passes Understanding

No one ever expected this woman to change the world, even her corner of it. She couldn't do what everyone expected her to be able to do. How could she make an impact on anything? Yet her prayers changed the direction that God's people were going.

It amazes me how matter-of-factly the Bible shares her story:

> Now there was a certain man of Ramathaim Zophim, of the mountains of Ephraim, and his name was Elkanah. . . . And he had two wives: the name of one was Hannah, and the name of the other Peninnah. Peninnah had children, but Hannah had no children. . . . And whenever the time came for Elkanah to make an offering, he would give portions to Peninnah his wife and to all her sons and daughters. But to Hannah he would give a double portion, for he loved Hannah, although the LORD had closed her womb. And her rival also provoked her severely, to make her miserable, because the LORD had closed her womb (1 Samuel 1:1, 2, 4–6).

A few sentences but it's a huge story.

"And he had two wives." Let's just stop there: Two. Wives. At. The. Same. Time! Just think about that. Because Hannah's name is listed first, we assume she is the first wife. We read that Elkanah loves Hannah. They begin their marriage in hopeful love, excited about the family they will grow. But months pass, and there is no child. The months turn into years. Years pass, and with them, the hope of a family. Hannah is not able to bear children. This is devastating. If you've struggled with infertility, you can begin to catch a glimpse of Hannah's life. You know what it's like to watch your friends bring babies home from the hospital while your house remains empty. You've shared in others' joy as girlfriends have gender reveals and baby showers while grieving the pain of your own dreams not coming true. You've had moments when it felt like everyone everywhere was pregnant except for you. You've felt like you wouldn't be able to handle one more baby shower invitation.

Hannah experiences this grief, but that is only part of it. In her world, women are expected to give their husbands sons. It is the thing that brings them value. The women who don't are looked down on and talked about. She has heard the whispers: "God cursed," and "must have done something horrible to deserve this." And she faces the sad truth that wives who don't have babies are replaced.

I can't even begin to imagine what that first night (or the later nights) was like when Elkanah brought Peninnah home. Second wives were culturally accepted as a way that husbands could get their much-sought-after sons. But imagine Hannah's pain on seeing the closed door, knowing her husband is with another woman—a younger woman—a woman who could give him what he most wants and she cannot. She feels the pain of not being enough.

Later, as Peninnah's body changes and grows, showing the evidence of a coming child, the tears and words of the enemy may follow Hannah. But it isn't just the enemy's words, "And her [Hannah's] rival also provoked her severely, to make her miserable, because the LORD had closed her womb" (verse 6).

"Rival." There is no denying what is happening in this home. These two women are rivals. Each wants what the other has: Hannah wants a child, and Peninnah wants a husband's love.

It seems that everywhere Hannah turns, she hears the message: She is a failure. She is not enough. God and her husband have given up on her. Yes, they love her, but they know she isn't good for anything. She can't go to the market without seeing the looks, hearing the whispers, or feeling alone and avoided. And now her own home becomes the place that hurts the most.

"Provoked her severely." Dictionary.com defines *provoke* as "to anger, enrage, exasperate, or vex."[1] Peninnah purposely wants to make Hannah angry, exasperate her, and not just a little but *severely*.[2] Picture Peninnah purposely, relentlessly, and meanly taunting Hannah specifically on the topic of her inability to have children. She is going after the most fragile, wounded place in Hannah's heart, much like the enemy does. Sometimes he attacks through our own thoughts, but often he uses other people. He does whatever he can to take out our hearts and destroy us, our relationships, how we see ourselves, and how we see God.

And it worked. "Therefore she [Hannah] wept and did not eat" (verse 7).

Now most of us lean toward emotional eating, don't we? We feel lonely, tired, depressed, or discouraged, and we head to our favorite sweet or salty snack. If we can't find that, anything will do. But this is a grief that drives Hannah beyond the ability to eat. Have you ever experienced anything so hard that even your favorite chocolate didn't look appealing?

The honest prayers of breaking hearts

"So Hannah arose after they had finished eating and drinking in Shiloh. . . . And she was in bitterness of soul, and prayed to the LORD and wept in anguish" (verses 9, 10).

Hannah's broken heart, her pain, and her feelings of not being enough motivate her to get up and go to God. She prays, but these aren't your nice church prayers. These are honest, gut-wrenching, angry, hurting, giving-it-all-to-God, crying prayers—the ugly crying and sobbing kind. She can't take it anymore, so she takes it to God. She lays it out. The Bible says "she was in bitterness of soul" and "wept in anguish." She was "a woman of sorrowful spirit"; she "poured out" her "soul before the LORD" "out of the abundance" of her "complaint and grief" (verses 15, 16). Can you picture the scene? Her heart?

She gives it all to God and discovers that He is enough. He is big enough for her pain, big enough to answer, and big enough to give her the peace that passes understanding (see Philippians 4:7). Afterward, "the woman went her way and ate, and her face was no longer sad" (1 Samuel 1:18). She doesn't get the answer that she wants yet—just the promise that God will answer. And that is enough for her. Peace and joy overflow her heart onto her face.

Hannah prays and discovers a God who is big enough for her not enoughness. A son is born, Hannah commits him and his life to God, and the Father uses her son to change the world. God again begins to speak and reveal Himself through her son. It's amazing what God can do when we pray honestly, giving Him our pain, our disappointments, and our not enoughness. That's when we discover that He is more than enough.

Finding peace

Jesus told His disciples to pray: "Pray, lest you enter into temptation" (Mark 14:38). The temptations would come. Prayer would bring strength and courage to resist the enemy. The disciples fell asleep, didn't pray, and failed to have the courage to face the battle and the fears that came their way.

Prayer is key in our daily battle, even with our battle of feeling like we are enough. It connects us to God. It gives God the opportunity to move and bless. He can do it without our prayers, but He is a God who respects people's choices. He won't impose or push. Prayer invites Him to do what He longs to do in our lives. Prayer takes us deeper and brings insights and wisdom.

Unfortunately, too many of us don't really pray. We pray blessings on meals, throw up a quick prayer on our way out the door, and fall asleep thinking about praying at night. Or we pray but basically see our prayers as our grocery list of wants from God. We pray for people when they're sick or need a job, but we don't always pray for the less obvious needs—the battles with attitudes and characteristics that need God's touch. We're more likely to pray for someone's physical healing than we are to pray for their salvation and more likely to pray that they find a job than that they find Jesus.

A friend recently told me that she was bored by her prayers. She prayed about the same things day after day. And if she was bored, what was God thinking, she wondered?

Too often, when we do take our concerns and struggles to God, we keep on worrying and struggling, never completely letting them go. We take them to God but keep our hands and minds on them too. We are prayer *worriers*, not prayer warriors.

Paul challenged people to pray differently. He outlines four steps to becoming a prayer warrior instead of a worrier and to prayers that promise peace: "Be anxious for nothing, but in everything by prayer and supplication, with thanksgiving, let your requests be made known to God; and the peace of God, which surpasses all understanding, will guard your hearts and minds through Christ Jesus" (Philippians 4:6, 7).

Let's dig deeper.

"Be anxious for nothing." Nothing. Not a thing. We can apply this to everything in our lives: kids, marriage, family, job, future, finances, health, and friendships. But we're talking specifically about how we see ourselves, our value, and our enoughness. That's part of this "nothing" too. Don't worry about yourself or about what others think. Don't be anxious about how you look, what you weigh, or what you accomplish. Paul isn't saying, "Don't think about these things or do anything about them. Do whatever." His challenge to us is not to be anxious about them. The *Merriam-Webster Dictionary* defines *anxious* as "characterized by extreme uneasiness of mind or brooding fear about some contingency: worried."[3]

When we focus on our not enoughness, we often worry about what people may think, what may happen, or how we may be perceived. But we don't really know. We tell ourselves stories that may or may not be accurate. Could the majority of things that we worry others think about us not be true? Maybe they're not even thinking about us! (They're too worried about what we're thinking about them.)

Be anxious for nothing. Is the Bible challenging us to never, ever be anxious about anything? In the original language, the phrase is written in the present tense. Paul isn't saying don't ever worry; he's challenging us not to live worried lives or focus on ourselves, our insecurities, our fears, and our doubts.

It's easy to say but harder to do. Luckily, Paul does more than tell us not to worry; he shares how.

"In everything." Oh, those little, tiny words! "In"—not before, not after everything has worked out but in the midst of. Paul challenges us not to worry right in the middle, when we don't know what's going to happen or how people will respond.

"By prayer and supplication, with thanksgiving, let your requests be made known." Paul employs four words that are all about prayer: Prayer. Supplication. Thanksgiving. Requests. Why does he use four different words to tell us to pray? Each one covers a different aspect of prayer. And if we follow Paul's lead, by the time we begin to talk to God about the worries that our not enoughness bring, we won't be anxious.

- *Prayer.* The Greek word translated "prayer" in Philippians 4:6 is always used with reference to God and a nuance of reverence. Paul is encouraging us to begin with worship, focusing on who God is and His character. We are to take the time to think about the One to whom we're approaching.

God invites us to "come boldly" before His throne, but let's recognize who we're talking to (Hebrews 4:16): He is the Creator of the heavens and earth and the Ruler of the universe. He is merciful, patient, loving, and relentless. He is our Warrior, Counselor, Provider, and the One who sees. Just taking a moment to really consider who God is will help to put things in perspective. It starts settling things down in our thinking and heart. You can't worry and worship at the same time.

- *Supplication.* A prayer of supplication asks God for something. Unlike intercession, which is praying for others, supplication is generally a request for the person praying. It's a humbling, begging, pleading submission of your will, which makes your heart *supple*, or soft. Supplication is a time to submit yourself, your will, your not enoughness, your too muchness, your fears, your worries, and even your dreams, your disappointments, your challenges, and your successes to God. You're giving them to Him much like Hannah did: honestly and completely. You're pouring yourself out and asking for God's will instead of yours, God's perspective instead of yours, and God's desires instead of yours. You're trusting that He who loves you more than anyone else wants more good things for you than you can imagine. You're trusting that He won't allow anything to harm you—possibly refine you—but never destroy you. Jesus' prayer in the Garden was one of supplication: honest, heartfelt, asking for a way out but submitting His will to God and trusting Him.

- *Thanksgiving.* Some people think we need to give thanks to God for everything that happens to us, including every difficult trial. But Paul doesn't say give thanks for everything. He challenges us to pray "*with* thanksgiving." There's a difference. I don't believe God wants us to give thanks for evil and the effects of sin. There have been moments and experiences in my life that I can't find anything for which to be grateful. These include moments that have brought pain and devastation and no apparent redemption. Yet I have always been able to find things for which to be thankful. That's what Paul is inviting us to do. Pray *with* thanksgiving. When a friend was angry and said hurtful things before walking away from our friendship, I didn't give thanks for the friendship ending, but I did give thanks that God will never walk away. When someone I loved struggled and made harmful choices and I felt helpless to do anything, I was grateful that God loves this person more than I do, *can* move in my loved one's life—and *is* working to draw this individual close even when I can't see it. Thanksgiving is another opportunity to focus on God, remember how He has led and provided, and remember His promises. As we battle our feelings of not being enough, we can be grateful for what God says about us and what He has promised to do in and through us. We can be thankful that He is enough, even when we're not.

- *Requests.* This is where we give God the things that are on our hearts. Talk to Him about the struggles—big or small. He cares about every detail in our lives. Nothing is too small. If it's big enough to make you anxious, it's big enough to take to God.

If we start with prayers that focus on God, supplication that seeks to submit to Him, and thanksgiving that resets our perspective, then by the time we give Him our requests, we will have peace and courage. We will remember how big He is and what He's capable of. We will trust Him and His love, knowing that He's big enough and loves us enough to handle whatever we bring Him, even our not enoughness.

But too often, we skip the first three ways to pray and jump right to bringing God our requests. We don't take the time to focus on who we're talking to, submit our will and seek His, or remind ourselves of what He's already done and promised to do. We treat Him more like Santa Claus, hoping He will give us what we ask. Then we walk away, continuing to struggle and doubt. We wonder whether He will answer. And if we're honest, there are times we really don't expect Him to answer.

"To God." When Paul says to make our requests known "to God," he's challenging us to stop looking at the "what ifs" and start focusing on the I AM. He's showing us how to turn our eyes away from our self-focus and insecurities—all the things that we're not enough for—and look to the One who is always enough. He's showing us how to come face to face with the God who loves us more than anyone else and has promised a peace that passes understanding, abundant life, indescribable joy, and boundless hope.

Warriors not worriers

God is challenging us to be prayer warriors, not worriers.

"When you hear the word *warrior*, what is the first image that pops into your mind?" I asked this question at a prayer conference where I was speaking. People responded with ideas of great soldiers: covered in armor, carrying a shield and sword, brave, big, and ready to fight.

But when I asked, "When you hear the words *prayer warrior*, what is the first image that comes to mind?" The image changed. Suddenly, people pictured little old grandmas praying for their families. Why does adding the word *prayer* as an adjective diminish what it is to be a warrior?

My friends, we are engaged in a battle *every single day*. We have an enemy out to destroy us. The Bible is clear on the imagery.

- "Be sober, be vigilant; because your adversary the devil walks about like a roaring lion, seeking whom he may devour" (1 Peter 5:8).
- "The thief does not come except to steal, and to kill, and to destroy. I have come that they may have life, and that they may have it more abundantly" (John 10:10).

- "For though we walk in the flesh, we do not war according to the flesh. For the weapons of our warfare are not carnal but mighty in God for pulling down strongholds, casting down arguments and every high thing that exalts itself against the knowledge of God, bringing every thought into captivity to the obedience of Christ" (2 Corinthians 10:3–5).
- "Finally, my brethren, be strong in the Lord and in the power of His might. Put on the whole armor of God, that you may be able to stand against the wiles of the devil. For we do not wrestle against flesh and blood, but against principalities, against powers, against the rulers of the darkness of this age, against spiritual hosts of wickedness in the heavenly places. Therefore take up the whole armor of God, that you may be able to withstand in the evil day, and having done all, to stand.

  "Stand therefore, having girded your waist with truth, having put on the breastplate of righteousness, and having shod your feet with the preparation of the gospel of peace; above all, taking the shield of faith with which you will be able to quench all the fiery darts of the wicked one. And take the helmet of salvation, and the sword of the Spirit, which is the word of God; praying always with all prayer and supplication in the Spirit, being watchful to this end with all perseverance and supplication for all the saints" (Ephesians 6:10–18).

It's time to put on the armor, pick up our shields and swords, and say, "No, I'm not letting the enemy win in my life anymore. He's not going to take out my heart and keep me from doing what God wants me to do or live the life God has called me to live."

God does not want us to live defeated by an enemy who hates us and is out to destroy us. He calls us to fight on our knees. Prayer is powerful as we lift up those we love and their needs and ours needs, too, but it is also a tool for fighting for our hearts as the enemy seeks to destroy how we see ourselves and how we see God. Worship, supplication, and thanksgiving—they bring a peace that passes understanding and "will guard" our "hearts and minds" (Philippians 4:7).

God's peace guards our hearts and minds—what we feel and what we think. It guards what we *feel and think about ourselves*. It guards what we *feel and think about God*. This peace that guards how we see ourselves and how we see God comes in response to our prayers; our intentional choice to focus on God, submit ourselves, and trust Him.

There have been moments when I've grabbed my prayer journal and pen as my heart battles. Discouraged, angry, and hurt, I begin to write, *Father God.* And before all the messy, battling thoughts come tumbling out, I turn to worship. Because I take time to begin with worship regularly, even on the hard days when I'm not thinking about it, my mind recognizes prayer and remembers worship.

Gracious God. Who extends mercy. Offers grace. Delights in us even when we are so messy. Patient. Kind. Who loves with an everlasting love. You are God.

The stormy, swirling emotions and thoughts calm. I sit in a moment of quiet. Looking out the window, I see glimpses of morning light begin to streak across the sky behind my neighbor's barn and trees. The outlines of goats and chickens start to come into view.

You know my selfish heart. Forgive me. Cleanse me from all unrighteousness. Keep me focused on You. Pour out Your Spirit. Give Him full authority over my thoughts and words, eyes, ears, and face.

The peace and calm deepen. I sip my tea and reflect on the day before.

Thank You for sunshine. For the sound of walnuts dropping outside my window. For crazy squirrel antics. Thank You for working it out for Rene to take the gift. For the things crossed off my to-do list. Thank You for sending the devotional from Celeste. For making sure the song was playing on both my CD and the radio so I wouldn't miss that You were speaking. Thank You for time with a friend. For Jennifer's willingness to be vulnerable and transparent. For Esther and Christine—so sweet and positive.

By the time I begin pouring out my heart to God, it doesn't feel like the world is completely falling apart. I remember that He is in control. I don't have to be.

God loves me. I can trust Him. So can you. He's got you. He believes in you. He's ready to help you fight.

Your story

- How's your prayer life? Are you taking the time to talk to God, really talk to Him every day?
- When you pray, do you leave your requests with Him? Or do you continue to worry about them?
- Have you had Hannah moments—when the pain was so great, you finally took it to God? What did you discover about God?
- How can you incorporate worship, submission, and thanksgiving into your prayer time?
- Are you beginning to recognize the battle for your heart going on around you? Can you see the battle raging for those around you too? How can you pray for them?

God is enough

God is enough for you to completely and honestly pour out your heart to Him and find peace.

Promise

"Now may the God of hope fill you with all joy and peace in believing, that you may abound in hope by the power of the Holy Spirit" (Romans 15:13).

Prayer

Father God, You are a mighty Warrior, and You fight for us. O Lord, forgive us for doubting, for being afraid, for worrying, and for asking but not letting go. Help us to trust You. Give us a glimpse of who You are and how You love us. Help us to find the courage to truly let go and focus on You. Stop the "what ifs" that run through our minds, and help us to focus on the I AM. Thank You for hearing our prayers, answering even before we call, and inviting us to come boldly. O God, help us to discover that we are enough in You and that You are enough for our hearts and minds. In Jesus' name, amen.

---

1. Dictionary.com, s.v. "provoke," accessed November 20, 2019, https://www.dictionary.com/browse/provoke.

2. Dictionary.com defines *severe* as "harsh; unnecessarily extreme." Dictionary.com, s.v. "severe," accessed November 20, 2019, https://www.dictionary.com/browse/severe.

3. *Merriam-Webster.com Dictionary*, s.v. "anxious," accessed November 21, 2019, https://www.merriam-webster.com/dictionary/anxious.

Chapter 16

There Will Be Days

The battle never ends—not until the trumpet sounds, and we are headed home. As we get closer to that moment, the enemy will ramp up and work even harder to steal our peace, kill our hope, destroy our relationships, and devour our confidence.

Not great news, is it? Sorry about that. It's the truth we live, but it's not the whole truth.

The enemy may try harder, but God will always pursue us relentlessly, grow us, draw us deeper, help us to fight the battle, and remind us of who we are in Him and who He is.

As we focus on God and His Word, we'll learn to believe more and more fully that we are enough because of Christ. We'll listen to and believe God more than the enemy. We'll faithfully trust Him and step into things that are too big for us to do without Him. We'll take every thought captive and make a relationship with Him the highest priority in our lives. We won't compare or compete but instead will care and connect.

We'll resist the enemy, and he will flee.

We're growing

There are days when I just shake my head as I remember the fearful young woman I used to be. I was the girl who sat quietly in meetings, afraid her thoughts and ideas weren't good enough to share. At events and social gatherings, I stayed busy in the background so that I didn't need to try to make conversation and talk with people. I always believed that everyone else could do things better than I could. I would walk into a room and assume that everyone was thinking critical thoughts about me, never anticipating that anyone would actually want to hang out and get to know me. I was a mess.

God wasn't about to leave me there. He loves me too much. He relentlessly pursued me with His love. I made knowing Him a priority in my life, and slowly, the fears faded. I'm no longer quiet in meetings. And a few people probably shake their heads a bit when I say, "I have this idea . . ." (I always have ideas.) I can walk confidently into a room of women and know that God loves me, He has a purpose for my life, and He has called me to love His girls. Instead of comparing, I look and listen for ways to encourage and affirm others and connect with them. I have confidence that He's called me to be me. Others may do the same things I do; they'll do them differently, but that doesn't make one way better than the other. There's plenty of opportunities for all of us. And I'm excited to know so many amazing women who are sharing God with others in their own unique ways.

But there are days . . .

There are days when I look in the mirror, and the old tapes begin to play. I'm not pretty enough, thin enough, educated enough, friendly enough, or engaging or interesting enough. I'm too talkative and animated.

There are days when I feel alone. There are moments when I wonder whether I'm making any difference in the world or whether I really have anything to offer. There are times when I wrestle with God, wondering what in the world He's doing. I doubt, and I struggle to understand why important prayers for people I love go unanswered.

We'll always have days when the battle rages strong and our hearts are taken out. We'll have moments when we doubt our worth or value and feel we aren't good enough. We'll have times when hope, joy, and courage are hard to find. The enemy will tempt us to doubt God is there or that He cares. He will try to get us to beat ourselves up, give up, hide out, and feel hurt and misunderstood.

We too often forget that we live in a battlefield and wonder why life is so hard. We grow weary. I don't know about you, but I'd like to win the victory and move on and never have to battle again. I want to live confident and secure all the time, never doubting and struggling. But I find that life doesn't work that way. We win the battle in one area of our lives, and the enemy attacks in another way. Or we're doing pretty well, resisting the temptations, and things are going smoothly. We recognize the enemy's tactics and steer clear of them, only for him to sideswipe us in a new way. As long as we are choosing God and growing, the enemy is not going to quit. And if we stop choosing God and stop growing, he'll try to keep us from all places, people, and opportunities that could draw us back into a relationship with God. He also will use God's conviction of the sins in our hearts to drown us in shame and guilt, instead of allowing God to lead us to repentance and freedom.

These are the moments when we need to keep pressing on. Understand that this battle is a journey, not a place we arrive and are suddenly always fine with who we are and where we're at, never struggling with life or doubting God. Get up, dust yourself off, and try again. There may be moments when all we can do is put one foot in front of the other and do the things we know will help:

- Connecting with God in some way every day—the one thing needed.
- Surrounding ourselves with friends who love God and love us.
- Battling to take every thought captive.
- Telling ourselves God's story about Himself, about others, and about us.

- Courageously stepping into things that are too big for us to do on our own.
- Cheering on others, and dreaming dreams for them.
- Offering ourselves grace when we fall, reminding ourselves that it's not the end of our story.
- Allowing God to speak into our sacred pain—not avoiding it, but letting it do the work God desires in our hearts and minds.
- Praying in ways that connect us deeper with God: worship, submission, and gratitude.
- Memorizing Bible promises that speak to who we are and who God is.
- Surrounding ourselves with reminders of what God says about us.
- Praising God, singing to Him, and getting out into nature and breathing deeply of its beauty.

It's not easy, but it's not easy to live in defeat, with discouragement, or by always beating ourselves up either.

Choose the hard way

We need to make hard choices about the way we're going to live.

It's hard to live in discouragement and shame.	It's hard to keep battling and reminding yourself of the truth.

Which "hard" way do you choose?

It's hard to live with the belief that you are hopeless and will never get life right.	It's hard to continually fight to take every thought captive.

Which way do you want to live?

It's hard feeling alone and rejected and thinking that no one wants to hang out with you.	It's hard to reach out and attempt to connect with people, believing that they might need a friend too.

Where do you want to be?

It's hard feeling like you have nothing to offer and will never make a difference.	It's hard stepping into things you know you can't do on your own, but you try anyway.

What do you want to do?

It's hard to look in the mirror and see all of your faults and all the ways you don't feel beautiful.	It's hard to look in the mirror and tell yourself you are beautiful in the ways God designed for you to be.

Who do you want to be?

It's hard feeling like you're not enough as a parent, wife, friend, or any of the roles you play.	It's hard reminding yourself and believing that God chose you for this role at this time because of who you are and what you bring to the table.

What do you want to believe?

It's hard to live in discouragement and defeat.	It's hard to fight for victory.

Choose which "hard" way you'll follow. It's your decision. And if you don't choose to battle, you've chosen to stay where you are. Even if you think you haven't made a decision or have told yourself that you don't want to stay there, then you've chosen. God is ready to fight for you and partner with you in the battle, but you need to take the first step. Decide to battle, then grab God's hand and resist the enemy.

I'll admit that I grow weary of the battle. Sometimes I don't want to fight, and I wallow for a bit in discouragement. Sometimes I feel like I don't have the strength. (That's because I'm relying on my strength instead of God's!) Sometimes I want to have a little pity party and feel sorry for myself. My friend Deb knows that life can be hard. She knows that there are days we don't want to battle, but she also knows we need to fight and not live in defeat. She encourages herself and others: "Feel the pain. But then get up and choose joy."

Choose joy. Choose to believe what God has promised—and promised *you*. Do the work. Pray. Get out your Bible. Turn on some Christian music. Go for a walk, and soak in the beauty. Start listing things for which you can be thankful. Call or text a friend. Remind yourself that you are loved and wanted by the King of the universe.

Moments of weakness

Peter knew about the battle. He'd lost a few himself. He challenges us, "Stay alert! Watch out for your great enemy, the devil. He prowls around like a roaring lion, looking for someone to devour" (1 Peter 5:8, NLT).

Can you picture it? Have you seen the National Geographic documentaries? The lion watches, quietly follows a herd of gazelle, and attempts to blend into the scenery, going unnoticed, while looking for signs of weakness—a gazelle wandering from the herd or a fawn that is tired and can't run as fast.

Our enemy is like that. He watches, waits, and looks for weakness. Peter says, "Stay alert!" He reminds us that there will be moments when we are weak, and the enemy will pounce.

Moments when we're physically tired. We can become depleted by too many late nights, too many early mornings, being up in the middle of the night, or by too many days of running nonstop and not taking time to rest. Exhaustion makes us prone to the enemy's attacks. God knew we'd need rest, so He created the Sabbath. Jesus often took time away from the crowds and took His disciples away to rest.

Moments when we're sick. I do not like being sick; most people don't. Sometimes when we're sick, we may be tempted to feel sorry for ourselves. We get frustrated with ourselves that we can't do the things that need to get done. We're not as alert. Maybe we're not hanging out with God and just want to sleep. Just as a lion will pounce on a weak or sick gazelle, the enemy will move in and attempt to take out our hearts when we're not feeling well.

Moments when we're struggling mentally or emotionally. We may be experiencing grief, not just for losing a loved one but any type of loss: a job, finances, or a relationship. Times of transition can also cause us to struggle: the kids move out, and the house becomes an empty nest; you retire, which is a time of excitement but possibly a time of doubt about how you'll find purpose and make an impact. Good changes—moving, a new job, getting in shape, losing weight, or having a baby—can bring joy but also questions that leave us a little off balance. A disagreement or fight with our spouse or anyone we love can make us feel upset. The enemy sees us struggling and moves in for the kill.

Moments when we wander away. Often the lion goes after the animal that wanders away from the safety of the herd, even if it just innocently strays to get a drink or a taste of sweet grasses. Our enemy watches for us to wander too. We might wander away from spending time with God, even innocently, when life gets too busy for a season. We still love Him and are committed to Him, but the urgent demands of life get in the way of real moments of quiet. We might wander away from church: we sleep late one week or get upset with the pastor or someone else in the congregation and decide we just don't want to go. We might wander away from friends who bring strength and courage. This tends to happen when we're struggling; we shut out the people we most need and hide out because we just can't face anyone. But sometimes life gets too busy, and we don't have time to meet for lunch or get together.

Watch. Stay alert. Take care of yourself. There will be days and seasons when life is crazy, and we'll be tired or struggle to make time for the most important things, such as time with God and with the people who love Him and love us. But we need to protect ourselves and make sure we're not living like this endlessly or for long periods of time. Say no to things, even good things, in order to say yes to what we most need: physically taking care of ourselves, rest, water, exercise, eating healthy (at least most of the time), taking time for relationships and connections, and offering ourselves grace when the going gets tough and we stop going.

The perfect storm

It was the perfect storm. I was exhausted physically, emotionally, and mentally. I should have seen it coming. But often when you're in the middle of a situation, you don't see how big the storm is.

I had spent weeks, months really, planning a big event: menus, speakers, music—all the little details to make women feel special and loved. I was working with a new hotel that had not held an event of that size before, in addition to processing the registrations and creating a team to partner with me. And I was also dealing with the crazy things that always happen, such as the fire alarm going off in the early morning (even for me) hours, waking those of us at the hotel the night before the event began.

Most details went smoothly, but there were glitches. My team was great, but they struggled with a group of people who were critical, demanding, and unkind to some of our other guests. I kept encouraging the team of committed women who volunteered their time to uplift and support those attending. The kitchen staff was new and didn't know the difference between a cucumber and a zucchini. (It was the first time we had ever had cucumbers on pizza, which didn't work for most of us.)

But there was more going on than just the event that weekend. There were big changes in my life and big changes at the office. A good friend was moving away. I was also presented with an opportunity that God seemed to be leading me to accept. Every prayer I lifted about it, as I sought wisdom, was being answered immediately. I prayed crazy prayers, wanting to make sure God was leading in what would be the biggest change I'd made in my work experience. It would require moving and learning a new role. (I love learning, so that was exciting to think about.) But it also meant that this would be my last event to plan in this location. I couldn't say goodbye to the ladies on my team because I didn't know what would happen for sure. But it definitely seemed like this would be the last time I would plan this event and gather with these women—many of whom I had known for years and years and I cared for deeply. They were the reason why I was doing what I was doing.

While busy with the weekend, I didn't always take the time to sit down and eat well. I often grabbed something quickly; when I did attempt to sit and eat, there was an interruption or problem that needed my immediate attention. So I wasn't caring for myself physically. I didn't get outside and breathe fresh air. I didn't have the opportunity to exercise, except to run up and down the stairs to my room.

I was physically tired and wasn't exercising or eating well. My mind was going in a million different directions as I supervised the event and tried to be present for people, in addition to thinking about the opportunity and changes that might be coming my way.

The enemy saw an opening, and he pounced.

He attempted to devour my trust in God. The door for the opportunity slammed shut in an incredibly painful way. I found myself hurt, bewildered, and blindsided. How could I have been so wrong about what I thought God wanted? Why did He answer so many prayers with affirmation and keep me walking forward, only for it to all come crashing down in an instant? Maybe He wasn't leading, and all of those things I thought were answers to prayer were just crazy coincidences?

The enemy sought to destroy my relationships. Someone who loves me ambushed me with incredibly hurtful words. I was devastated and numb.

The enemy used others to try to steal my confidence in God's calling for my life. Reeling from both events, I opened my email when I returned to the office, only to find critical, hurtful emails from someone who had been at the event. These emails complained about me as a person—not the event or my team. They told me how great my team was but then listed the things wrong with me as a person.

I was devastated.

I questioned myself, God, the call on my life to serve His girls, and my ministry. It felt like every area of my life was in chaos, and I was reeling.

But I chose the hard way. Instead of letting the enemy take out my heart, I battled back.

I clung to God, dug into His Word, claimed promises, worshiped, praised, and prayed honestly. I told Him that I didn't understand everything that had just happened, especially with the opportunity I truly believed He had opened to me. (I still don't understand. He and I spent some time talking about it before sharing it here. But I'm committed to choosing to trust Him over understanding.) I made sure to spend time with Him and not hide out from Him in shame, thinking I had blown it. I chose to trust Him. If He had truly wanted the new role for me, He could have made it happen. He didn't, but He had a plan. He loves me. I can trust Him.

I asked a couple of trusted friends to pray. I've learned from experience what happens when I hide out and cut myself off from friends. It's not pretty or healthy.

I got up and got out. I went for walks outside and took in the farmland that surrounds our home. I ate healthily and went to bed on time.

I looked for things for which I could be grateful. I played a song or two on repeat in my car—songs that gave me courage and reminded me of God's love.

I took every negative, beating-myself-up thought captive and told myself a new story. I reminded myself that God loves me, delights in me, has a plan for my life, and has called me to serve Him.

I prayerfully responded to the emails. I shared them with my boss and was encouraged by his support.

I put one foot in front of the other and just did what I could to battle the enemy and trust God each day as I walked through the storm.

And you know what? He brought peace, courage, and joy right in the midst of the pain and devastation.

Were there ways I had failed? Yes, but I was not a failure. Were there things that I wish I had done differently? Absolutely. But I can trust God with His plan. He loves me more than anyone. He knows me better than I know myself. He wants more for me than I want for myself.

Victory

I know what we'd love is a complete victory. Honestly, I'd like God to zap me and never let me doubt Him or my enoughness again. But victory is more than winning once and for all.

Victory is resisting every time we look in the mirror and hear the tempting words that we're fat or not pretty. It is reminding ourselves that we are fearfully and wonderfully made.

Victory is swallowing our fears and stepping out anyway, reaching out, speaking up, doing the hard thing, and trying something we may not succeed at accomplishing.

Victory is choosing to push past our doubts and just try something new. It is speaking up in a group and sharing our thoughts. It is trusting God, even when we can't see Him doing anything.

Victory is getting up late and missing our time with God but not beating ourselves up. It is finding another few minutes later in the day or talking to Him on the way to work instead of listening to the radio or calling a friend.

Victory is telling ourselves a new story when the enemy tempts us to believe that we are not enough, that someone doesn't like us, that someone wouldn't be interested in us, and instead pushing past and reaching out in friendship.

Victory is saying, "Thank you," instead of diminishing a compliment.

Victory is not giving up.

Your story

- Where are you at with the battle? Are you recognizing the enemy more often? Resisting him?
- How do you respond when you've been doing well, but you suddenly hit a wall and struggle?
- What are the ways that work best for you in resisting and battling the enemy?
- Do you recognize the need to care for yourself physically, emotionally, and mentally so that you're stronger for the battle? Are there changes you need to make in your life in order to care for your body and mind better?
- In what ways have you had victory this week?

God is enough

God is enough even when you get it right one day and wrong the next.

Promise

But this I call to mind,
and therefore I have hope:
The steadfast love of the LORD never ceases;
his mercies never come to an end;
they are new every morning;
great is your faithfulness
(Lamentations 3:21–23, ESV).

Prayer

Father God, Ruler of the universe, the One who sees all and knows all, You know us, even the number of hairs on our head. And You love us with an everlasting love, drawing us with Your loving-kindness. You know that there will be good days and hard days. There will be days when we trust You, and days when we can't seem to hear You or find You. There will be days when we battle strongly, and days when we just want to give up. Thank You that through it all, Your love never fails. Each new day brings new mercy, grace, courage, and hope. Father, we put our trust in You. Give us courage in the storms. Help us to be alert, recognize the enemy, and run to You! In Jesus' name, amen.

Chapter 17

One Day Very Soon

One day very soon the battle will be over. We already know how it will end. The enemy will be destroyed. God's beloved children will be home. God wins.

How I long for that day!

Some of you may not be quite as excited. Yes, you want to be a part of it, but you are afraid you're not enough for heaven—not good enough or accomplished enough—and you aren't doing enough. My desire throughout this book has been for us to learn and believe that faith is not about us being enough. It's all about God. We are not enough on our own. We cannot make it to heaven through our own goodness or by doing enough. The only way to heaven is through Jesus Christ.

Many try to make themselves be enough or do enough or prove themselves. Jesus warns us what will happen in the end to those who think they can do these things by themselves: "Not everyone who says to me, 'Lord, Lord,' will enter the kingdom of heaven, but only the one who does the will of my Father who is in heaven. Many will say to me on that day, 'Lord, Lord, did we not prophesy in your name and in your name drive out demons and in your name perform many miracles?' Then I will tell them plainly, 'I never knew you. Away from me, you evildoers!' " (Matthew 7:21–23, NIV).

Jesus makes it clear. It isn't about what these people have done. They have done a lot of great things. But being good enough or doing enough isn't what gets you into heaven. Did you catch what He tells them: "I never knew you"? It's not about what they have done; it's about who they know. It's about a relationship. Are we growing in a relationship with God and trusting Him? Are we relying on Him to be enough instead of ourselves?

Contrast this with another story Jesus told about a group of people who also come to Him in the end:

"Then the King will say to those on his right, 'Come, you who are blessed by my Father; take your inheritance, the kingdom prepared for you since the creation of the world. For I was hungry and you gave me something to eat, I was thirsty and you gave me something to drink, I was a stranger and you invited me in, I needed clothes and you clothed me, I was sick and you looked after me, I was in prison and you came to visit me.'

"Then the righteous will answer him, 'Lord, when did we see you hungry and feed you, or thirsty and give you something to drink? When did we see you a stranger and invite you in, or needing clothes and clothe you? When did we see you sick or in prison and go to visit you?'

"The King will reply, 'Truly I tell you, whatever you did for one of the least of these brothers and sisters of mine, you did for me'" (Matthew 25:34–40, NIV).

For this group, it was never about being enough or doing enough or getting it right. These people didn't even realize all that they had done for Jesus. They did what they did because they loved Him and because He had gifted them and called them to care for others—not so they could be enough but just because He loved them.

It's not about what we do. It's not even about all we do in Jesus' name. It's Christ alone who makes us enough. Trust Him. Make knowing Him a priority—the one thing you need to do every day. Take the time to pray prayers that aren't just sharing a wish list but conversations that draw you deeper, worshiping Him, submitting to Him, and being honest before Him. Pray grateful prayers that worship Him for what He's doing and how He's caring for you. Let His story about you be the one you believe and tell yourself. Don't give up on yourself or beat yourself up, even when you sin and fall down and make a mess. Just bring it all to Him, confessing, asking for forgiveness, repentance, and healing. Watch how He redeems. Walk through the sacred refining pain, believing that while it's hard, He's right there with you and has something better for you on the other side.

Don't let the enemy take you out by telling you that you're not enough. Remind him and yourself that God is enough and, one day very soon, He's coming for you.

The promise

One day the earth will shake. The trumpet will sound. The sky will fill with angels. We'll feel ourselves lifting off the ground after the graves will have opened, and we'll see people whom we have missed as they meet Jesus in the air. Unseen angels who have always been here, protecting us and watching over us, will suddenly be visible. Their faces will be filled with excitement and joy. The day they've been waiting for is here! Finally, they'll be able to reveal themselves to us. They'll tell stories of how they protected us and will ask us questions about what it's like to know Jesus loved us so much that He died for us.

Other angels will come, bringing babies and children and returning them to the arms of their parents. There will be laughter, surprises, and tears. Our minds will struggle to grasp what's happening. *Really? Is this it? Is Jesus coming for us? Are we finally going home?*

Then we'll see Him—Jesus.

He'll be coming in the clouds with the angels. His smile and joy will radiate an excitement that will fill the universe. A shout will fill the air that will echo for eternity.

I'm not sure how Jesus is going to do it, but I believe that when we look at Him, it will be as if He's looking directly at each one of us and we will look right into His face and see the love, the joy, and the delight.

Angels will guide us as we fly for the first time. We'll go to meet Jesus in the air, speechless, with tears of joy running down our faces. The world and all of its pain and battles will fade behind us as we hear Him say, "Welcome home! I'm so excited! I couldn't wait for this day to finally arrive and for you to be with Me forever!"

We can only imagine

Picturing the moment of Jesus' return brings tears to my eyes. I don't know what it will be like, but I love to imagine it and think about it. It fills me with hope. As we travel through the universe to heaven and arrive at the place He's been preparing specifically for us, I doubt our brains will be able to take it all in. There will be so much to see and experience: loved ones reuniting, being near Jesus, seeing the angels, traveling through the universe, and arriving in heaven where God and His host are waiting. The banquet table will be ready and waiting. There will be more beauty than we have ever seen or experienced—and there are some amazing places in the world.

Yet even as we imagine what Jesus' return might be like, our human experience and thinking cannot create a complete visual for what it will really be like. It will be "exceedingly abundantly above all that we ask or think" (Ephesians 3:20). The Bible promises,

> "No eye has seen, no ear has heard,
>   and no mind has imagined
> what God has prepared
>   for those who love him"
> (1 Corinthians 2:9, NLT).

We will spend eternity learning and understanding more of this God who loves us so incomprehensibly. We will sit at His feet, worship Him, listen to His teachings, and note the way He looks at us—with such love and delight. And maybe every now and then, He'll burst out singing over us a song that we've never heard but that feels so familiar.

We'll build friendships with people, such as Hannah, Peter, the Samaritan woman, Martha, David, Esther, and others whom we've only known through pages of the Bible. We'll listen to them tell about all the things we didn't know. And they'll be excited to hear *our* stories. What was it like to have the Bible as a resource so many years after Christ walked the earth? We'll enjoy sharing with family and friends how God worked and what happened after their deaths. I look forward to introducing my dad to my now-grown sons and their wives. He loved them so much and would be proud of them. And I know he'll absolutely love my daughters-in-law Kat and Sarah. Oh, and I'll tell him about my writing and speaking. He will believe the writing part of my story but not the speaking portion. The woman he knew would never have had the confidence to travel and get up in front of people.

We'll meet people that we've read about or knew from a distance—pillars of faith whose stories inspired us and challenged us. We'll discover stories that we never heard before about people we knew. It will bring an understanding of their lives and personalities on this planet.

And all of this will happen without the enemy's audio track playing in our hearts and minds. We will have no insecurities, no feelings of not being enough, no overthinking, and no comparing and competing. I look forward to that while not really being able to imagine it.

The you that you were created to be

Without the enemy's accusations and lies, God's truth will be the only thing that defines us. We'll finally believe and live as the people He created us to be. The fears, doubts, insecurities, pride, and selfishness will all fall away. He'll complete the work He began in us—each of us. We'll get to know the people we love as the people God created them to be. And we'll live more fully as the people He created us to be.

I love the Christian classic *Hinds' Feet on High Places*; it tells the story of Much-Afraid, who has twisted feet and lips and who lives in fear. One day the Shepherd invites her on a journey to the High Places. He gives her two companions to help her as she climbs the mountain trail: Sorrow and Suffering. The journey is hard, and she often feels like giving up or thinks she'll never make it. She learns to submit her will to the Shepherd and trust Sorrow and Suffering to do the refining work of sacred pain in her life. At the end of the story, when she reaches the High Places, the Shepherd gives her a new name—Grace and Glory. Her companions transform too. They are now Joy and Peace. The Shepherd asks her what lessons she's learned from her journey. She shares several. They are lessons we, too, will learn—and are learning—on our own journeys. As we reach heaven and begin to comprehend more fully God's love for us, we, too, will realize what Much-Afraid does: "The third thing that I learned was that you, my Lord, never regarded me as I actually was, lame and weak and crooked and cowardly. You saw me as I would be when you had done what you promised and had brought me to the High Places, when it could be truly said, 'There is none that walks with such a queenly ease, nor with such grace, as she.' You always treated me with the same love and graciousness as though I were a queen already and not wretched little Much-Afraid."[1]

My friend, one day—and I believe it will be very soon—our lives and battles here will make much more sense. The battle will be over. We will look into our

Father's eyes, and His love will consume and overwhelm us. We will finally believe that He loves us just as we are, even though He never intended to leave us that way. He *has* always been working to refine, draw, and heal us. His plan was always that His love would make us whole and holy and transform us into the daughters that He designed us to be. And when He speaks our new name over us, we will realize that He's seen us that way all along (Isaiah 62:2, Revelation 2:17; 3:12). While we have struggled with our not enoughness, He never has.

Your story

- Do you ever think about what Jesus' return is going to be like? Do you ever imagine what heaven will be like?
- When you think about Christ's return, are you excited or afraid? If afraid, what are you afraid of? What does the Bible say? Who is speaking these fears into your thinking—the enemy or God?
- What are you looking forward to about heaven and living on the new earth?

God is enough

God is enough for eternity.

Promise

"For the Lord Himself will descend from heaven with a shout, with the voice of an archangel, and with the trumpet of God. And the dead in Christ will rise first. Then we who are alive and remain shall be caught up together with them in the clouds to meet the Lord in the air. And thus we shall always be with the Lord. Therefore comfort one another with these words" (1 Thessalonians 4:16–18).

Prayer

O God, we believe Your truth and we doubt it. We're excited and we're afraid. We long to see You, but we wonder whether You will accept us. Father, forgive us for believing the enemy over Your Word. Help us to fill our thoughts and minds with Your promises and believe You. You are coming for us. You want us to be with You for all eternity. You love us. You know we're not enough, but that's not how You see us. You see us as the daughters You created us to be. Give us the courage to trust our not enoughness to You and believe that You and Your love are enough. In Jesus' name, amen.

---

1. Hannah Hurnard, *Hinds' Feet on High Places* (Wheaton, IL: Tyndale House, 2003), 241.

Invitation

Thanks for sharing this journey with me. I'm praying for you. I don't know your name, but God does. I'm praying that you'll find the courage to accept God's invitation

- to stop focusing on your not enoughs and focus on the God who is more than enough;
- to attempt new things, try things that are impossible to do on your own, risk failing or looking silly, and discover more of Him;
- to discover the God who doesn't leave, beat you up, or shame you when you fail and mess up;
- to leave behind doubt, fear, and unbelief and to trust this God who loves you more than anyone ever has or ever will, dreams bigger dreams for you than you can imagine, and created you for such a time as this;
- to let your not enoughness cause you to discover the God who is enough.

I'd love to hear from you—hear how God is leading, the too-big things He's challenging you to do, the new stories you're telling yourself, the things you're learning about Him as you choose the one thing needed, and the ways you see Him using you and growing you. Email me at daughterinawe@yahoo.com. Please note that I'm not a counselor, just a girlfriend who cares and loves to hear stories about how this amazing God is loving His girls and making them whole and holy.